George W Miles 1982
700 E. Arbor st. SP 401
Long Beach Ca. 90805

Positive Fishing

THE ART OF ANGLING

YOUR OUTER LIMIT

Positive Fishing

THE ART OF ANGLING
YOUR OUTER LIMIT

Robert G. Deindorfer

SEAVIEW BOOKS

NEW YORK

First Edition

Library of Congress Cataloging in Publication Data
Deindorfer, Robert G
    Positive fishing.

    1. Fishing.   I. Title.
SH441.D44   799.1′2   79-67600
ISBN 0-87223-660-9

FOR MY BROTHER JACK

"Remember that angling is an art, and an art worthy the knowledge and practice of a wise man. He that hopes to be a good angler must not only bring an inquiring, searching, observing wit, but he must bring a large measure of hope and patience, and a wit and propensity to the art itself."

Izaak Walton

Contents

Positive Fishing

THE ART OF ANGLING

YOUR OUTER LIMIT

Preface

O N A FAMILIAR TURN in a river I fished back in my boyhood I once came upon a rumpled man laden with more fish than the state of Illinois allowed, which offended me not so much because of his inability to count but because I had yet to land my first fish despite a long day fanning the river with assorted plugs and live baits.

Since I was far too young to be a fish and game warden, the transgressor never hesitated as I stood there watching. He swung his bait-casting rod again, pitched a flashy red and white spoon into the water, and made an agreeable sound when a big bass I would have given a week's allowance to catch boiled up to feast on the spoon. He played the fish for a few tingling moments before it broke off, and expressed none of the profane regrets customarily used in those circumstances. Easy come, easy go.

During a brief conversation on the riverbank the rumpled man admitted that, yes, it had been a good, if not a spectacular, day for him. He added that he seldom failed to get his share of fish, a singularly inappropriate way of describing such forbidden numbers, I thought, and then disappeared beyond some willows toward a concrete bridge, presumably in quest of still more, which I had little doubt he would manage.

I encountered the same angler again a week or two later. On that occasion he was carrying a canvas bag instead of a stringer, which seemed more discreet, but an alarming bulge in the bag suggested he might have some explaining to do in case a warden appeared, as happened just often enough to keep most local anglers relatively foursquare.

After he twirled the spoon out one last time, I couldn't resist asking if he would share some of his secrets with me. He seemed delighted. Although he half-heartedly deprecated my judgment that he was the best fisherman on the Fox River, he seemed to know virtually everything there was to know. The two of us sat in the twilight, talking, talking, talking, master and apprentice, teacher and pupil, Piscator and Venator.

He talked bass, catfish, carp, and panfish; talked plugs, spoons, spinners, and baits; talked sinkers, bobbers, and lines; talked promising holes in the river, talked for perhaps an hour before he suddenly fell silent. He sat for a little while, brooding, his face screwed in a mask.

"Fishing calls for something else, too," he said finally.

"What's that?"

In the folds of my memory I can see him still. He dramatically cocked a long index finger, dramatically tapped it against his forehead. "Find the right groove," he said. "You've got to lose track of everything else."

Briefly, very briefly, then, I had a dim glimmer that there was more to fishing than patience, casting ability, and the pick of the shelves at Crosby's and Fagerholm's sporting goods stores. But I was young, young and innocent, and the full weight of what he meant eluded me for a long time. Now that I am no longer young, and my innocence lies in tatters, I know how much more there is.

Since that far-off evening in Illinois, when I was mostly arms and legs, several other perceptive sportsmen have helped open my eyes to a special concept of angling not found in outdoor magazines or fishing books. Since then my priorities have turned inside out. Like the most thoughtful among them, I am not so preoccupied with technique, not so obsessed with the fine print of the literature, that I can't see, out beyond the bends in the mind, that misty plane where pure, positive fishing is to be found.

It is not the purpose here to discuss the mechanics of the double haul cast, the advantages of trolling a large sucker for muskie, or just how to rig a plastic worm for big bass at night, except as they relate to the outer mental limits of the sport. My charter is Positive Fishing, not technique.

But let there be no misunderstanding. Any angler who can develop greater mechanical proficiency, more technical knowledge, and a proper feel for the water will be all the better for it, provided these accomplishments do not intrude on the subliminal forces waiting to be tapped. As Buck Rogers, the celebrated Missouri angler, writer, resort owner, and guide once said, "It isn't really necessary to hit a fish in the eye at thirty yards, but it helps."

Besides, technique in all its infinite detail is covered in the abundant literature devoted to the sport. Whole books have been written on crank baits, on walleye pike, on exactly how to fish the nymph. In his impressive two-volume work on trout, Ernie Schwiebert describes 20 different rise forms. Another angler I know wrote a full text on nothing except leaders, length, strength, taper, knots, the lot, which, mercifully, never saw the light of print despite the fact that he kept sending it off hopefully to publishers. The amount of esoterica available in the bookstores is almost enough to make a person swear off reading, or fishing, or perhaps both.

The vital psychological components that enable anglers to fish their absolute outer limits apply to the sport in all its popular basic forms. These components are no more restricted to fly-fishing than to swimming live frogs in hopes of bamboozling bass or pike.

Unfortunately, too many sniffish fly casters look down on other types of fishing as less subtle, less challenging, less satisfying. Although they seldom say so aloud, these angling snobs imply that their own specialty requires more intelligence, which can sometimes suggest social graces and the good life.

"An oaf can put a maggot to a hook but to comprehend the greater pleasure of the fly a man has to stretch his brain," a recent article in a fly-fishing journal stated.

In demeaning live-bait fishing on the grounds it calls for less skill, the author exposed an awkward lack of understanding, which seems too prevalent among anglers who confine their shopping to Orvis or Hardy Brothers. It's perfectly true that an oaf can skewer a maggot on a hook and catch fish, sometimes a large number of fish. But it's equally true that an oaf can knot a fly to a leader and hoodwink trout, bass, or even salmon.

Fly-fishing requires a different order of skills, but the skills themselves are no more complicated. Any type of angling can be as simple or as complicated as a participant wants to make it. The fly caster needn't be aware of the five advantages of Left Hand Line Acceleration to enjoy himself; the spin fisherman can land pike without being intimately aware of their spawning cycle.

Richard Carr, for example, a prize-winning English match fisherman whose approach to his sport is every bit as creative as that of some thoughtful brother of the angle who prefers flies, goes to extremes that stretch the brain to the breaking point. In his voluminous logbook he often even lists just how deep his fish were hooked.

On the day I watched Carr compete he arrived at his beat trundling a two-wheeled trolley heaped with nine rods from 10 to 18 feet long, 11 reels, endless boxes of hooks, weights, and floats, tins of maggots, casters, and meat, not to mention three bread loaves intended to victimize fishes, if the situation seemed to suggest it.

One box was so abrim with floats only slightly different one from another that I couldn't help but comment on the plenty. "More than a hundred in the case, I reckon, different types, most of them, made from drinking straws or peacock feathers. Beautiful floats, too, if I do say so," Carr remarked before he explained how the most sensitive of them could detect the slightest peck at his bait.

During the match he stopped speaking altogether, shoveled special formula-ground baits into the water, and changed floats, hooks, weights, baits, rods, and reels like a man possessed. But he also admitted to drawing on resolve, concentration, feedback, and other inner resources that enabled him to make those changes instinctively and with no conscious effort.

8

The fact that Positive Fishermen like Richard Carr bring such a subtle inquiring mind to the kind of angling they most enjoy would have pleased Izaak Walton. Although elitist dry-fly purists squirm any time they are reminded of it, Walton, the father of us all, a distinguished non-oaf and a successful biographer and poet, liked nothing more than ground-baiting water the night before he fished it with—horrors!—maggots, minnows, or live frogs instead of the artificial flies cast by many antique contemporaries.

Finally, some acknowledgments are very much in order here. In addition to thanking my wife, Joan, and son, Scott, who forgave me my domestic lapses while this book was in progress, I am especially indebted to Brooks Roberts, a Positive Fisherman with a wonderfully positive view generally; to Bob Portner, fisher and friend; to Ned Morgens, Hig Manning, and Emil Peters, who fish the same home waters; to several brothers of the angle here and abroad whose personal experiences help illuminate the far side of fishing.

But most of all, I am indebted to my father, who is gone now. On many a special Wednesday afternoon and Sunday he used to drive me out to fish the Du Page, Turtle Rock, or Pistakee Bay, the Maumee or the mud lakes of Indiana. I've caught a lot of fish since then, more than my proper share, I suppose, salmon in Wales, trout in Austria, bass in Arkansas, big pike up along the Canadian border. But I would trade every last one of them for another night fishing bullheads with my dad on Blackberry Creek.

Robert G. Deindorfer
New York City
Mid-season 1980

[I]

Positive Thinking:
The Vital Difference

BACK IN A QUIETER, simpler age American rivers and lakes thrummed with fish. Bass and pike, bluegill and crappie, perch and pickerel, trout and even salmon were so plentiful that even a duffer could fill up a stringer or creel.

Dated accounts of especially memorable catches illustrate the prodigious returns to be had way back when. Fifty years ago two men fishing strictly for the pot landed 127 trout in Minnesota one summery day; a Georgian took his legal limit of bigmouth bass in less than an hour; a teenager caught almost 100 pounds of fish jugging a Mississippi backwater. In Morrison, Missouri, the catfish that four grown men heaved onto a freight scale came to an astonishing 312 pounds.

Unfortunately, that abundant age is over and done with. Polluted waters, more power dams, impoundments, and other obstructions, insufficient state and federal funding, water skiing and recreational boating, an ever inflating number of anglers—54 million at last count—have all contributed to relative hard times. Celebrated fisheries as diverse as Maine's Allagash

River, Center Hill Reservoir in Tennessee, Wisconsin's Flambeau, and Miramar in California have all suffered.

That same distressing trend is in no way confined to American waterways. In a competition I fished in England's River Lee 55 contestants caught a total—a total, mind you—of just 15 legal fish during a five-hour match. Elsewhere, New Zealand's Tongariro River, Loch Leven in Scotland, and Austria's Lake Traun are among all too many troubled waters producing fewer fish.

None of this ought to imply that freshwater fishing is in any danger of becoming a minor sport. It isn't. Over a long period of years it has gotten too great a grip on the public for that. But, like so much else, fishing isn't what it used to be in terms of total volume, which is how participants generally measure success.

Despite the diminished supply in relation to demand, a limited number of men and women consistently out-perform everyone else. It isn't difficult to identify these specialists. They're the ones catching the most fish, and having a happier time of it, too, or, in most cases, both.

Whether they use spinning tackle or fly rods, troll from boats or swing lazybones cane poles, these people amount to a breed unto themselves. Although they generally fish the same waters with much the same type of gear, they somehow manage to bag more fish than others, who have done as many or even more seasons on the water.

North and south, east and west, these trophy anglers run up bulging inventory figures for reasons some of them can't quite explain themselves. For example, in January of 1977 Dick and Elaine Hengl, two certified Bassmaster virtuosos from Iowa, commenced fishing the tail waters below the lock in Florida's Lake Toho in hopes of hooking enough to write home about. The two of them weighed in the first 20 fish they conjured up, a total of 148 pounds, one of them 11½ pounds, four over 10 pounds, six others over eight pounds, a bonanza even by their own impressive standards.

Run-of-the-millstone anglers nourish wistful day-dreams of someday hooking a three- or four-pound trout the taxidermist can mount for the rumpus-room wall, but trophy anglers like Trevor Hously regularly scale their dreams to larger sizes. Unless a fish runs well over five pounds, Hously doesn't consider the day especially memorable. Memorable days tend to blur some in Hously's mind, but he won't ever forget the morning his three trout scaled eight and a quarter, nine, and nine and a half pounds.

Like it or not, an inequitable percentage of game fish fall to a very few people. According to the manager of Indiana's Willow Slough State Fish and Game area, just 12 out of more than 22,300 visitors accounted for more than 90 percent of all the fish one recent season, while four monopolists took an estimated 85 percent of the smallmouth bass in a lake in Michigan that attracted hundreds of anglers.

On the basis of similar creel and stringer counts that same trend applies in Bull Shoals in Arkansas, Lake Jackson in Florida, and on Flaming Gorge in California and Utah. Less than 10 percent of American anglers land somewhere between 85 and 90 percent of all the bass, trout, pike, and other game fish hoisted out of our rivers and lakes. In the case of our single largest sports fish, the muskellunge, the percentages run higher still.

Even the rare busted days when these high-volume producers fail to bring in their normal quota have a way of healing over. If for some baffling reason they don't connect with a respectable fish, they are convinced that it won't be long before they do. Their buoyant confidence is contagious.

"I didn't have a bass, not one buster bass, all night long, but it didn't worry me any, except I knew the boys working the dock would kid me when I checked in," Otis Vaughn, a fast-talking mountain man who fishes Lake Norfork in Arkansas, once remarked. "I know the secrets—and I knew it wouldn't be long before I was in business again. Next afternoon I had seven bass, up to seven and a half pounds."

At the risk of exposing my own occasional defects I

can't help but cite a bittersweet case in point out of my own experience. Several years before I uncovered the subliminal, almost mystical gifts these anglers employ I was fishing the classic River Test in England with my customary results, modest, quite modest, only an occasional trout to my rod. Yet half a mile behind me Ernie Schwiebert, a master whose skill is almost impossible to describe adequately, was hooking trout on every third or fourth cast even though he was working an alien piece of water, too. Altogether, he hooked and released more than 20 trout, one of them so substantial I went weak in the knees watching him release it.

Schwiebert, Vaughn, Hously, the Hengls, and others may have little in common apart from their astonishing catches and the freemasonry endemic among those who share a special, high-intensity concept of angling. Individually, they vary considerably one from another. They go up and down the age scale, live in different parts of America, come from different walks of life, fish different waters for different fish.

Even the whimsical old cartoon we have seen in all its endless variations—a gentleman angler who looks as if he's stepped straight out of the pages of the Orvis spring catalogue, and a small rural boy, barefoot, freckled, clad in tattered jeans, with a primitive cane pole and a can of worms, the former empty-handed, the latter lugging a great beast of a fish—is less comical than it might appear. In many ways, a youngster is every bit as close, perhaps even closer, to the whispering nuances and secrets of the sport than an adult who has become freighted with too many rigid habits.

The fact that the great bulk of game fish fall to so few anglers suggests that there is far more to fishing than simply pitching a popular brand-name lure into a convenient sheet of water, which is perfectly true. As originals like Lee Wulff, Edward R. Hewitt, Richard Walker, Homer Circle, Ed Zern, and others learned for themselves, serious fishing is a creative act, subtle and sometimes profound, a challenge to stretch the mind. Yet even when it takes on the perplexing shadings of the Barbetski Formula it remains a leisurely, pleasurable sport transacted in the magnificent realm of the outdoors.

The cerebral aspects of fishing certainly did not escape the notice of the single most celebrated person ever associated with it, Izaak Walton, whose *The Compleat Angler* has been a perennial best-seller ever since its publication in 1653. Although the affable English Royalist wasn't infallible—Atlantic salmon don't spawn in April and May, for example—his guidance was generally quite sound. Walton and the more perceptive contemporary anglers frequently emphasize the advantages of cerebral and psychological factors without ignoring basic layers of skill. In an innovative, split-level new era, aspiring fishermen might just as well also have the best rods and reels, the most bamboozling assortment of lures, flies, and baits, the most practical nets, books, and incidental equipment they can afford, although the recent article in an outdoor magazine listing the 34 different items a participant ought to have in his vest, not counting several boxes of flies, strikes me as absurd.

The more proficient an angler becomes at casting, tying nail knots, blood knots, and other relevant hitches, learning how to read the water, the greater his prospects, depending on other instinctive and subconscious factors whose total impact contributes beyond any measure.

It takes something other than mere skill techniques to become a truly compleat angler. I know a man, an outdoorsman, whose casts are like shooting stars. He works an incredible length of line, miraculously casts under low branches along the river edge, feathers a small dry fly to delicate landings just where he wants it, a picture caster, a model who could pose for those how-to photo sequences in the instruction manuals.

Despite that rare gift, despite an easy-does-it schedule that allows him a long season, however, my friend has a major flaw. He just doesn't manage to catch many fish for an angler of his travels and experience. He's caught not many fish on the Au Sable and the Gunnison, the

Itchen and the Hampshire Avon. He once went two tormenting days without so much as a single trout while several companions whose casting didn't compare with his had a weekend littered with fish.

Fishing amounts to both more and less than the mechanics. Being a good, if not a spectacular, caster is a cheap skill we can all learn fairly easily and practice mechanically, but to fish well is not a cheap skill, or any kind of skill at all, really, and there is no place it is taught except in the pools of an individual's mind, as the relatively few men and women who produce the most fish have discovered.

Exactly what accounts for the success of these super anglers? Why do they consistently catch more fish, pursue the sport with such brimming confidence, enjoy themselves more than less fortunate brothers of the angle? After all, they appear little or no different than someone drifting in the next boat or wading the next turn in the river.

More often than not they even use much the same basic tackle, cast similar lures, flies, or live bait, fish the same rivers and lakes during the same soft times. Experience isn't really a factor. Some of them have fished for a long time, but others have fished for only a few seasons, and still others are so new to the sport that they have yet to wear out their first reel.

What separates the rare super anglers from millions

of other frustrated and humbled Americans is something that isn't found on the shelves of a tackle store or in the hash marks on the sleeve of a fishing jacket. It's an approach, a program, a concept that seldom meets the eye. At its higher levels the approach becomes so acute that devotees are not even aware of why they fish as they fish.

Whether they realize it or not, however, they are tuned to a different emotional wavelength. Some of them hit on it by themselves while others heed the advice of anglers who already have found the secret. Even anglers seemingly locked in by barnacled habits that restrict performance find it deceptively simple, provided they manage to open their minds and stretch to the outer limits of their angling experience.

Once outdoor Americans move into this new realm there is seldom any return to the less productive, less satisfying days of yore. They have stepped through the looking glass. They have reached into the evolutionary, productive, flowing realm of Positive Fishing.

[2]

Positive Examples of
Positive Flow

SOME YEARS AGO A BRASH, convivial personality named Al Henderson bought a general store in Wisconsin's rolling lake country. As a storekeeper he sold quantities of bread and other staples to locals and outlanders without allowing anyone to run up excessive bills. Nobody, not even Henderson himself, ever ranked him much more than a routine businessman.

It wasn't commercial success that caused Henderson's reputation to filter far beyond the boundaries of his town and attract strangers from various parts of the state. The general store was strictly incidental. As countless people came to discover, Henderson was a fisherman, a marvelous fisherman, perhaps the best fisherman in a part of a state addicted to the sport. If he wasn't the best by definition, he was at least the most successful, which may be better still, a blunt fact illuminated by the large bass, pike, trout, even muskies mounted on the walls of his store after he pulled them out of neighboring rivers and lakes.

For years, Al Henderson caught enough trophy-sized fish to stock an aquarium without falling on the prolonged lean times that so often beset so many anglers.

He fished whenever he had the chance, night and day, in good weather and bad, isolated, alone, part of the landscape, singing scraps of old songs to himself, thoroughly contented on the waters he loved. Throughout the lake country he was regarded with a respect approaching awe even by experienced fishermen.

As the season approached its end Henderson used to fish harder than ever, working a favorite cove on a lake, a promising riffle of river, a small stream that might produce trout, until it was finally over for the year, except perhaps for a few days of ice fishing, which he didn't like all that much but helped him through the winter. As he left his last waterway for the season, not to set foot on it again for months and months to come, he experienced his moments of private sentiment. He'd pitch out another cast, take a last lingering look at the river or lake as the sun melted down and autumn began to color.

But the sport isn't ever really out of season for Henderson. During the winter, over the bumps of the long short-lighted months, he cleans and oils his reels, varnishes and mends rods, sorts through his tackle box, feeds on the sweet memories of trips gone by, dreams dreams of even sweeter memories still to be caught and scooped into the net of his mind.

How does Al Henderson do it? How does he manage to consistently perform far better than other seasonal anglers who fish much the same tackle, use many of the same lures and baits, fish the same waters, even wet their lines at approximately the same time? How?

It is never easy to focus on exactly what sets a virtuoso apart from others who participate in the same creative act, which serious fishing is by its very nature. Whether it's Paderewski playing the piano, Nureyev doing a *grand jeté,* or John Le Carré magically casting a spell in another novel, the art form is partly private, inner-directed, something that cannot be bottled or graphed or fed into a computer. Yet in Henderson's case, the basis of his phenomenal success is no great secret.

Although he didn't fully recognize all the nuances himself, he was a Positive Fisherman, a Positive Fisherman of the first rank, a self-taught master who found new dimensions of the old sport. He fishes outer limits beyond the reach of most other anglers simply because he has hit on several components that, if not especially difficult to employ, were not simple to combine properly.

As a Positive Fisherman, Henderson learned how to improve and increase those psychological elements important for anyone who wants to consistently fish wisely and well. Wherever he fished, whatever freshwater species he pursued, he went into a familiar drill that helped him establish the proper tempo, stretch his confidence and concentration, spin a useful feedback drum in search of the most effective technique, approach, or tackle for the challenge at hand.

But more than anything else, Henderson, like many another genuine Positive Fisherman, achieved the emotional high known as *flow* while he was out on the water. Given that acute state of concentration and pleasure, his reflexes, skill, and knowledge were all enhanced to a point where he fished with greater proficiency than he would have otherwise. In many instances success corresponds to the degree of flow an angler achieves, which can vary depending on both tangible and intangible factors.

"I get myself in sort of a groove," Henderson once told me. "I'm happy and enjoying myself and I can feel the groove growing. Sometimes I get so wound up that I almost forget it's me catching the fish. I see the fish, see it jumping and thrashing and being pretty well handled. It's funny, but I'm not always sure it's me on the other end of the line."

During those times when a fisherman, an athlete, an artist, or almost anyone truly enjoying whatever it is he's doing experiences the soothing sense of flow, his skill, perception, and performance improve. The more consumed a participant becomes in spinning out beyond the limits of self-consciousness, the better he is likely to perform. Ballplayers sometimes speak of special moments when they are playing out of their minds, beyond the rim of their talents, in a zone they have trouble explaining later. Almost invariably those special moments unfold when they are feeling a happiness close to exaltation.

Once anglers arrive at a state of flow they think it might last forever and they'll go right on selecting the perfect bait or fly, casting exactly where they want, hooking fish without committing a lapse, their concentration and confidence soaring. It doesn't last forever, indeed sometimes not even from one day to the next. It may not even be at the same intensity, although there are ways of both initiating and prolonging flow.

Anxieties and a sense of daunting challenge tend to inhibit natural flow, for example. This is especially common among beginning anglers, whose nerve ends tighten because the sport seems so bewildering the more they hear. If fishing becomes too easy, the fish themselves too plentiful, too simple to hook, too defeated while they are being played, boredom may also take over. And boredom stifles flow just as much as anxiety does.

"The domain of flow is the band between anxiety and boredom," says Daniel Coleman, an authority who has observed its impact on different activities and recreations. "An alert mind resists boredom by keeping us involved in events around us. A relaxed body is the physiological opposite of tension. The two together—alert mind, relaxed body—combine to make us ripe for flow."

What makes fishing especially susceptible to flow is its basic simplicity. If there are fish to be caught, we either catch them or we don't. Despite an abundance of instructional literature that sometimes becomes bewildering, the goals themselves aren't difficult to understand and fishing isn't hedged in with excessive snarls of rules, regulations, and red tape.

If fishing as a sport lends itself to flow, not every devotee can attain it. The pleasure and attendant improvement are generally beyond overly competitive anglers who fix foolishly impractical goals. However they might manage to raise a simulated self-confidence that keeps them going, anglers who set these impractical goals—a limit of bass in less than an hour, a catfish big enough to break the state record, a 10-pound trout on a 6X tippet—become so antic, so tense, so frustrated that flow suffers.

An experienced Positive from Lafayette, Indiana, used to feel the pleasurable surge regularly until he lifted his sights too high. During a long woolly night in a bar he made the mistake of betting a friend $25 that he would catch a 10-pound bass that season.

Although I have had no personal experience of them, sad to say, 10-pound bass are possibilities, however remote, provided the waterway an individual fishes holds an occasional fish that size. Unfortunately for the sake of this Positive, such wasn't the case. He spent the summer fishing a grid of small mud lakes around his part of Indiana, relatively productive lakes on their own terms, actually, with smaller bass, bluegill, perch, catfish, and other standard-issue Indiana fish. Unfortunately, however, there was never once a recorded bass of more than eight pounds, two ounces, and that fish had been caught many years before.

Moody, irritable, easily distracted, his confidence at a low ebb, this poor Positive nevertheless pursued that phantom target like Captain Ahab, fishing late into the night, abandoning his family for entire weekends, a driven angler chasing a 10-pound, $25 bigmouth bass. Before he finally paid off the bet, he noticed that his concentration had fallen off, his casting and judgment had suffered, his whole attitude had begun to tilt.

"I'm not fishing happy any more," he complained to a friend.

"But you're still fishing."

"Yes, but it isn't the same. When I'm not fishing happy I feel a lot different. When I'm fishing happy I fish better than I should. Things go better."

In the opinion of others who experience the same pleasure, that Indiana angler wasn't exaggerating. Things generally do go better when a sportsman is feeling a sense of flow. In its strong form I have seen flow improve the hand/eye contact important in both hooking and playing a fish.

Flow has also been known to induce a curious state of identity. Ade Scutt, a prominent British match fisherman who makes a specialty of catching an astonishing number of tiny bleak in hopes that their total weight will win a tournament, admits to becoming so immersed in the assembly-line process that he sometimes loses track.

"After a while I go numb," he says. "Sometimes it isn't me whipping those fish off the water. I don't know who it is, but it isn't really me."

Anglers who hope to maintain a positive surge of flow have developed tricks to help it along. A bass fisherman on Lake Miramar in California goes into a preliminary meditation, a lady in Tennessee persuades herself that she always will have a hit the very next cast, and a withered insurance broker who fishes the Wye in Wales visualizes the next fish he will hook and kill. Participants in search of greater flow are restricted only by their own imagination.

More and more Positives aware of the value of flow divide a day on the water into fish modules in an effort to keep the vibrations going. Even when fish are coming fairly easily, they give themselves a time-out every two or three hours. The technique doesn't work for everyone, especially anglers riding such a pleasurable high that they lose track of time, but it has a beneficial impact on many.

Yet flow isn't always something to be switched on and off just like that. It should occupy time at both ends of the fishing day. For example, the drive home after a day's angling is a comfortable period to let the flow continue. It is evening and the headlights cut long cones through the dark. There might be some good fish in the trunk of the car and there are moments to savor. An angler may wistfully reflect on a big one still rising, still mocking him when the twilight faded, coming close without ever quite taking, gently reminding the angler that he wasn't as good as all that, or at least not just then, anyway. This is as approximate a time to achieve that positive flow as in any pre-angling conceptual exercise.

Several persons who are aware of experiencing flow while they fish feel that it never disappears altogether. Even when they stay away from the water for three or four weeks the flow is still there to be tapped, a warming sensation that gives fishing more bounce.

The multiplying effect of flow on less skillful, less experienced anglers is not to be ignored. Once an angler starts catching fish, flow can accelerate surprisingly quickly and reach levels that stretch individual limits. Unless the fish come so regularly as to induce boredom, the more good fish a person catches, the greater the degree of flow, until, at a certain point, that misty feeling may be achieved.

At that ultimate point when the angler is totally captivated by the sensation, so hooked himself that realities around him fade, strange things can happen. In California, trophy fisherman David Zimmerlee says he once talked himself into a nine-pound bass he couldn't even see. Yet the fish he hooked and netted scaled exactly nine pounds.

A bespectacled Positive Fisherman named Jim Beebe looked into heavy waters at Lake of the Woods in Minnesota, saw and described three fish nobody else in his party could even see, and then proceeded to hook and land all of them.

The eminent old English angler A. H. Chaytor once claimed that he frequently found he could practically call his shots with salmon. In his flow-induced vision the fish appeared closer, more detailed, almost bigger than life. In such circumstances it wasn't difficult for Chaytor to tell himself he would hook a particular salmon in the left or right side of the jaw and then do exactly that.

The experiences of Chaytor and others might sound improbable if they existed in a vacuum. They don't. Athletes in other fields have made similar observations about their own enlarged awareness during times of acute concentration. Baseball players riding hot streaks speak of the ball appearing larger, golfers describe the cup as mysteriously expanding as they line up a putt, one professional quarterback seriously told of throwing passes to a receiver's thumbnail. Hall of Fame slugger Ted Williams, a thoughtful man given to fascinating reflections on batting, said he sometimes could actually see the seams on a ball hurtling at him at more than 90 miles an hour.

In his earlier, more visible incarnation as a college and professional basketball player, United States Senator William Bradley used to achieve a flow so intense that it measurably sharpened his awareness. He didn't do anything special to switch on the flow that contributed to his coordinated, balanced game. After he'd been playing for a few seasons it became a part of his normal game, another piece of equipment he couldn't do without. In a major tournament game in which Bradley scored more than 40 points as a collegian, he wasn't even aware that he was having such a big night. As he explained to a sportswriter later, he had been caught up in a high-intensity spell that enabled him to dribble, pass, shoot, and do other things beyond his normal superb abilities. During that spell, he performed great feats with only a hazy notion that he himself was the individual who kept drilling the ball into the basket.

After Bradley began playing basketball on a full-time

basis that same sense of flow intensified until it occurred almost every time he stepped onto a court. In a way, the most impressive demonstration of his flow came not in an NBA championship series, although he played in several, not in some dramatic showdown game, although he participated in his share of those, nor even on a night when he personally shot the eyes out of the basket. The most impressive single instance of how flow can enlarge awareness may well have come about on the day he walked onto a New Jersey court for the first time to go through a brief workout. He positioned himself in a familiar spot on the floor, a bit off to the right of the keyhole, 20 feet or so from the board, and lofted several one-handed shots at the basket. When those shots hit the rim instead of whispering through the cords, as generally happened with practice shots from that particular spot, Bradley's formidable eyebrows arched some.

The practice gymnasium was strange to him, but the unities of the game were locked in his instincts. Given the normal degree of flow that developed when he so much as picked up a basketball, Bradley was keenly aware of the width and length of the court, the condition of the floor, the backboard, hoop, and the ball he was shooting. On the basis of those first experimental shots Bradley suspected that something was wrong.

In a quiet way, without complaining or offering any

excuses, he remarked that the basket appeared to be an inch or two higher than the regulation 10 feet. While the possibility seemed unlikely, a stepladder and measuring tape were produced to determine whether the suspicion was accurate. As things turned out, it was, by a matter of just over an inch, a trifling difference, really, unless a person happens to shoot baskets for a living.

The same magnified awareness, that same improbable sense of dimensions, is often experienced by Positive Fishermen who manage to achieve a substantial flow. It enables them to fish at their absolute outer limits by casting more accurately, using more hair-trigger reflexes, and concentrating to a point where they actually tune out what might seem to be overwhelming distractions.

"Often it is difficult to realize that one's flow is running up the scales," James Ford, an ardent angler and golfer much interested in the positive process, has said. "It is difficult because one can reach a point where it seems normal. But when it isn't functioning, or it's receding, it becomes immediately apparent."

Ford is an overwhelming talker, passionate and voluble, especially on the matter of flow, a man in search of exactly the right words to express the glow, the satisfaction, even the ecstasy to be had. He is convinced that the difference between an average weekend fisherman and a superior one amounts to no more than that pleasure zone.

"A person can have a great time of it at a number of different things, golf, bowling, squash, even playing a kazoo, I suppose," he said. "What makes fishing so special, what gives fishermen more pleasure even when they aren't producing is flow, flow and the environment in which we participate."

Ford paused before elaborating. "If for any reason the bowler, the squash player, even the kazoo freak is not having a good day, he has no reinforcing fallback position," he said. "There he is enclosed in a smoke-filled alley or a compound consisting of four concrete walls or perhaps the same old living room. But the environment in which we transact our sport can lift the spirit, and add to the natural flow for concrete results."

No angler would quarrel with Ford's view. Fishing is the quiet sport it was intended to be. The background music makes pleasant echoes. In a place where all is still, the slightest sounds—the hiss of a line, the plink of a lure hitting the water, the whine of the reel—can be nicely deafening.

Fishermen have acknowledged the healing qualities of the recreation ever since Walton cast a lyric reference book upon the centuries more than three hundred years ago. "For those poor rich men, we Anglers pity them perfectly, and stand in no need to borrow their thoughts to think ourselves so happy," wrote Walton, who appeared to fish in full flow himself. "No, no sir, we enjoy a contentment above the reach of such dispositions."

That sort of mood can do more than arrest any serious counterflow when things aren't going as well as they might. It can also help generate a faster, more forceful flow, which often becomes progressively more advanced. Eventually it can become so consuming that the participant performs feats he wouldn't believe he was capable of.

A curious memory flickers in Carl Popovich's mind any time he falls to brooding on the effect of flow. Years ago the big southern Illinoisan was fishing a backwater in Arkansas. He was fishing it with the such phenomenal success that he eventually lost count of the bass and crappie he was landing on a spinning rod.

"The thing was spooky after a while," he recalls. "I was fishing the same way, using the same lures, fishing a lake I'd fished before. But when they got to really hitting I felt this strange sensation. I thought I'd had too much sun. I had no feeling of time. The hours slipped by before I knew it, click-click, like a movie run at high speed. I made longer casts than ever before and played fish without a mistake."

At the time he finally packed up for the day Popovich was startled when he checked his watch. It read 8:15 P.M. He'd been fishing since ten that morning without so much as a pause for lunch or the Thermos of coffee he'd brought along—or at least he remembers no such pauses. At a guess he figured he had fished for an hour or two, successfully, because he was aware of all the fish at the time he was catching them.

Some anglers fishing the outer limits of flow are convinced they can cast any distance, hook any fish, play even massive fish on light tackle. At least one of them has inverted the classic equation, and sees the fish actually competing for the lure or bait.

"I think not of fishing for salmon but of letting salmon fish for me," George Jarre once said. "There is an invaluable lesson in looking at it that way."

To hear some Positives tell it, there is also an invaluable lesson to be learned in focusing on old, far-off times. According to these people, an angler who has trouble turning on a proper volume of flow need only recall to mind some favorite river or lake from his youth.

All right.

Even at a distance I can see it now, the Fox River, lighted with sunshine in a world simple and quiet. There was water to fish then, gurgling water spilling over a dam below the Tivoli Theater. There were fish to be had, bass and carp, sunnies and catfish, once in a great while even a throwback garfish, memories, every one of them.

The last time I visited, water washed over the dam still, but it was foul, streaked with oil and crusted in spots, a river down on its luck. It is sad to think that the Fox River as I knew it is gone, that it no longer holds an intriguing supply of fish, and that youngsters the improbable age I myself once was can no longer pull something out of it. But rivers can be like the flow required for someone to fish those tantalizing outer limits. Rivers fluctuate, rise and fall, are subject to change with little or no notice, too.

[3]

Technique:

Keep It Quiet

EVER SINCE SOME ANONYMOUS ENGLISH ROYALIST elec-
trified his old-fashioned contemporaries by catching the very first fish on rod and reel, anglers in general
and American anglers in particular have been preoccupied with technique. There is far more to the sport
than that, or at least there is if a participant's priorities
are in reasonable order. Unfortunately it seems that
sometimes this truth gets buried under a layer of
incidental how-to twaddle.

For one reason or another game fishing's commercial
gurus can't quite bring themselves to acknowledge the
fact that too much attention paid to form can seriously
affect substance. Many newspaper outdoor columns,
fishing magazines, and angling books contribute to the
general emphasis on technique. Over and over again
we are faced with information on how to tie knots, how
to manipulate a fly, bait, or spinning rod, how to pick a
backlash apart, change spools on a reel, string a plastic
worm on a hook. In my opinion, there is nothing quite
so much fun as a stack of that kind of reading, except
maybe a leaky wader.

In an effort to justify all the newsprint, all the hardcover books, and all the teaching seminars devoted to the care and feeding of better technique, management generally goes into an awkward little preface saying tut-tut, no matter how long a fisherman has been at it he still needs to improve his casting, and, well, practice makes perfect. Right. Meanwhile Positive Fishermen, who put their mind to more important matters, are out emptying the waterways of more fish than anyone else.

Back in the bittersweet time before I discovered the pleasure of fishing my ultimate limits, I sunk myself in the same morass most anglers find themselves in. On what looked a rainy day when the river I originally planned to fish was experiencing ominously low water, I once decided to stay in the cabin boning up on a book that virtually guaranteed to turn the reader into a tournament-class caster in five easy chapters.

"That's greasy kid stuff," a friend chided. "You may get all hooked up with the do's and don't's and forget the important things."

Off he went, emotionally weatherproof, a big gruff man carrying a lovely Orvis rod and a pocketful of dry flies, clumping toward a sweet river in felt-soled size 12 waders. As he explained to me later, after I had tried to untangle the riddle of the perfect roll cast in that easy-does-it book, he had had a lovely time of it for more than an hour, fishing in a light rain, fishing in his old effortless way, taking two small trout, plus an intriguing big brownie that broke off on the far side of a submerged log. So much for belles-lettres.

"Casting technique!" His mouth opened in a wide grin. "Once you really get fishing you can forget casting technique."

In the literal sense of his words, my occasional angling companion was being altogether accurate. Positive Fishermen who've done their apprenticeship can indeed forget technique. In the Catskills and in Wisconsin, on the salmon rivers of Iceland and catfish backwaters in the deep South, nothing is as important to these experts as a wider overall focus, with casting and other mechanics reduced to secondary instinctive behavior.

Over the years weekend anglers who aspire to a Positive status must distinguish the important from the not-so-important. Fishing being both simpler and more complicated than it might seem, men, women, and children have to guard against the hazard of becoming preoccupied with the less essential (because mechanical) aspects of the sport.

The gap between mechanics and experience is substantial. No matter how well a person learns to cast, feather a fly onto a quiet pool, or retrieve a plug at the most tantalizing place, he will never arrive at his potential until he learns to sublimate the emphasis on perfect technique, to stop counting to himself, to let the whole act become natural and instinctive.

Some years ago Tiger Joe Garland, a big, broad-beamed professional football player, turned from his crunching sport, or vice versa, to civilian life. Among the other features of his leisurely now-career, he gradually began to do some bass fishing on a small lake just outside his back window in central New York. After reading a few manuals, listening to several friends who fished, watching a shoal of youngsters spraying the water with casts, Garland decided to teach himself.

"It was like learning how to drive a car," he recalled later. "I was clumsy and fumbling for a while, but then something clicked and it came naturally. From that moment on I have been casting fairly well with no real effort."

Exactly. Until anglers lose their obsession with technique, in spite of years of experience, they remain wrapped up in secondary matters and overlook what it's all about. Technique must be used, of course, but always subliminally, hidden away below in the rim of the mind, never rising quite to the surface, useful and on tap strictly as reflex movement.

As D. D. Sceats and several others have observed, technique amounts to presenting a fly, lure, plug, or live bait in such a way that the target fish will take it into the mouth. Fishing success and failure are largely bound up with that question of approach. It is too easy, too simple, too tempting to make the mental leap from technique to fish—and thus mistakenly to think technique is what catches fish. Sadly, for the sake of too many anglers, this isn't so.

Instead, it is the fly itself, the lure, the plug, or the bait that catches the fish, and they only work if the fish can be prevailed upon to snap at it. Therefore, technique is not connected directly to the taking of the fish but only to the offering of whatever is at the end of the line.

Nothing corrupts more promising anglers than a self-defeating obsession with technique: from any form of casting, for example, although casts differ and the degree of required proficiency varies, to tying the most intricate fly. Fishing books and magazines are littered with detailed directions on, and illustrations of, exactly how to do it, with the images as homely as possible—driving a nail high into the wall, throwing a baseball, looping a line over a tree, that sort of thing. These will produce a capable angler. I aim to instruct a school of thought based on taking capable anglers and using them to their highest angling potential.

As many anglers know, the rudiments of fly casting can be learned in an hour or so. All a beginner has to do is observe a competent caster for a little while, pick up a rod, get the feel of it, move it in the prescribed arc, one-two-three, let the line roll until it tugs slightly, bring the rod vigorously forward to a ten o'clock position and let the line gently fall on the water. Instincts are wonderfully useful.

While basic casting is in no way challenging and need only be practiced until a sufficient ability is achieved, the abracdabra, the mystique, and the endless talk of forward tapers, shooting heads, and other lines frequently keep anglers so conscious of what they are doing that they never file the mechanics away as something they have mastered and can perform in a spontaneous way.

The true Positive treats whatever type of casting he does just like he treats other mechanical phases of the sport. He does it instinctively, without really considering it, with no sense of self involved. Once he succeeds in developing the required detachment, other essential positive components—confidence and concentration, feedback and flow—rise to the surface.

The more thoughtful Positives regard their casting arms as separate units, not quite part of them, forever flexing, forever pausing, forever whipping forward, the whole sequence a reflex action, something to be observed and regarded in an impersonal, third-person sort of way. I suppose every so often this can lead to a certain bemusement.

One day I stood watching an angular old Positive fishing a lovely piece of water on the River Colne just outside of Bibury in England, after taking an oh-boy look at some five- and ten-pound trout crowding a pond in a nearby hatchery. It was a pleasant afternoon, warm and sunny, filled with birdsong, I was fishing happily, with a bagged sausage roll and a tin of ale on a nearby bank to sustain me.

"You're casting beautifully," I called out when he dropped his fly almost on the nose of a rising fish.

"Yes, he's casting quite well today, thank you, isn't he," he replied.

Although they manage to keep casting technique and other mechanical skills subordinate, Positives do have some tricks that improve performance and help reach their outer limits. Given an especially long, daunting cast, the average angler frequently considers the distance until, in the end, he becomes so spooked that his cast is not more but less than normal. In case a bait rod is involved, the torment might well be compounded by a snarly backcast, from which even the best anglers suffer.

Without any conscious effort, Positives approach the same situation differently. Ignoring the distance, they focus on a particular bulge in the water or on a weed patch, and shoot directly at that. A spin caster in Maine refused to believe that he had hit the near side of a log three consecutive times because, upon looking over the water later, he considered the distance far beyond him.

Submerging the awareness of casting and other techniques is admittedly difficult. Yet it is only by keeping Positive priorities intact that fishing will improve. How-to directions, like fishing fantasies, need to be left at the water's edge.

Even the fundamental act of eventually netting a fish after it has been played out must remain no more than a reflex, to be transacted with little or no awareness. Aside from the desire to land the fish before its time has come, the reason so many are lost in that final phase is largely a matter of the angler losing spontaneity, becoming too preoccupied with technique when he sees his prize rolling in the water only a few feet away.

But even the most spontaneous Positives realize that the game is not yet up. A sudden surge, a slack line, a badly frayed leader, a hook working loose, even a shallow bottom offering some leverage can all cost an angler dearly if he isn't careful. In the blunt words of an old Irish proverb, it is not a fish until it is on the bank.

Instead of using the net in an instinctive fashion, without conscious effort, they are all too mindful of the mechanics. Hesitant, less certain, they swing the net rather than leading the fish to it, miss, swing again, feel a flutter of panic if the fish skids away at the last moment. As the spontaneous air of detachment dwindles, they become desperately involved, which can be even more defeating. In case the fish happens to be big or loosely hooked, or not what Walton described as "a leather-mouthed fish," it may well escape due to such fumbling. Inept, progressively more futile attempts with the net by amateurs have long been the subject of whimsical conversation among their betters. At the Antrim Lodge in Roscoe, New York, I recall the night several anglers got to competing with one another recalling stories of especially comical moments they had witnessed.

"I can't forget a great lump of a man trying to land a small bass on the Current River in Missouri, slapping at that poor fish like a collector waving a butterfly net." The angler spinning the worn memory shook his head. "He knocked off the bass, knocked off his whole rig, tipped over, and fell in the river. Last thing I saw was his net floating down around a turn, which may have been just as well, for all the good he made of it."

If an authentic Positive consciously thinks of anything at all during the final act of landing a fish, it often has to do with nuances, shadings, peculiarities, which register as the angler calmly and surely goes through the old drill one more time. An especially bright color, a scar, even a defective fin, any one of a number of features, might make this fish a little different from the last. And before a Positive can panic, the fish is safely in the boat.

This view helps provide the protective undercoating that enhances concentration, confidence, feedback, and the degree of total flow required.

"It doesn't matter whether I'm drawing a bigmouth bass or a flathead catfish into the net," a veteran Positive named Frank Grugett of Oklahoma City says. "It's another fish I've beaten, netted with no last-minute heroics, although naturally I use more care with bigger fish."

Grugett and others resist the tintype images of particular fish not because they are less interested in species, but because they know that a wider outlook contributes to the detachment that is so much a part of Positive Fishing. So they preserve this wider outlook during the final rites, netting a satisfying fish effortlessly, without becoming really involved. This is an essential but in no way transcendental part of the total flow of fishing the outer limits.

This is not to say that some of the more advanced Positives have not developed special netting techniques of their own. They have. The bald, cheery New Yorker who writes and angles under the whimsical pseudonym "Sparse Grey Hackle," for instance, has managed to reduce his theory into reflex. It has long been Sparse's opinion that the reason a trout takes on a frantic new life just when it seems most negotiable is the startling sight of a strange white hand manipulating the net, which he therefore goes to some trouble to hide.

Other anglers working the Catskills and the huge southern lakes have hit on innovations of their own. California's Claude Borman shortened the handle on his net until he was almost holding it by the ring for greater control, while Bill Mueller of Ann Arbor, Michigan, built himself a funnel-type net which he finds more secure.

"A really good angler isn't opposed to more effective technique or innovation." Mueller spread his hands in a gesture of explanation. "But a really good angler is opposed to self-conscious technique that intrudes on total experience."

Minor adjustments are sometimes necessary, of course, but Positives have learned how to fix the priorities, how to achieve free flow in netting a fish, or in doing any other required but mechanical aspect of the sport.

That matter-of-fact approach applies to sharpening hooks, tying knots, stringing lines and leaders. Anglers in flow perform these essentials spontaneously, concentrating and feeling a proper surge of confidence as the mechanics become as automatic as blinking an eye.

A young English stockbroker walked a track along the River Itchen, walked past a shed where several others sat sharing a packed lunch. Beyond a stand of willows the river turned left (as did the stockbroker), widening some, spilling over a small stone dam. In hazy sunshine a trout showed in the riffles, a good trout of perhaps three pounds.

Quickly the angler dipped into a wide pocket in his jacket, pulled out a plastic box, extracted a Pale Water Dun, in a size 18, which he had successfully fished many times before. He clipped the lame duck fly off the light 15-foot leader, spun the Dun onto the tippet. To a visitor who happened to be following upriver, it looked as if he had changed flies without so much as taking his eye off the magic spot where the fish had dimpled.

"How many loops did you use knotting the fly to the leader?" the visitor asked.

"How many loops?" The angler didn't turn his head as he considered the question. "I have no idea. I don't keep count of such things. More than enough, of course, but let me see."

He held the rod high, got hold of the fly again. "Seven loops," he said. "I had no idea just how many. I tend to do these things in an incidental manner, don't I."

The visitor was a flagrant non-Positive. He fished rigidly by the book, generally turning to watch his backcast unfold, making certain he swung the rod no farther than the one o'clock position, and going to great lengths to put exactly the same number of loops in the knot he used to attach the fly. This time, his faith shaken, he stood there long enough to watch the stock-broker collect a dividend that weighed three pounds and two ounces on the pocket scale.

Anglers who have slipped the normal moorings and moved far offshore frequently are not aware of the fiddly essentials they endlessly perform, which enable them to demonstrate not only the form but also to achieve the results they seek. They find habit and experience beneficial, and the best of them hook, play, and land more than enough fish to prove it.

Even the blank challenge of night fishing fails to ruffle a Positive's spontaneous detachment in the matter of technique. Angling by night instead of by day obviously calls for a slower, more deliberate beat, which Positives pursue with leisurely instincts. Some mid-western anglers working big sheets of water in the dark do preliminary calisthenics simply to tune up their reflexes. Hal Bosworth occasionally wraps a handker-chief around his eyes and fishes blind for a few minutes in the afternoon to prepare for the dark.

Bosworth nearly tipped himself out of the boat just

past midnight once, and he admits to a certain frustration trying to pick through an occasional backlash. Yet his technique is so reflexive, the nocturnal experience such a demonstration of self-enforced Positive attitude, that he spends a lot of time on the water after sundown, with impressive results.

It wasn't so long ago that he came in out of the dark of the night with something more than a feeling of great contentment, Hal Bosworth the consummate Positive Fisherman had filed another notch in a crowded memory. He came in out of the dark lugging a bass, a special bass he won't ever forget, the biggest bass of an epic career, 10 pounds, 7 ounces, a thick, sullen shape now hanging on his office wall.

[4]

Positive Rhythm:
The Right Beat

D URING A PROLONGED CONFERENCE with an American intelligence officer of lofty rank the two of us got to talking a subtle and fascinating aspect of tradecraft that seldom surfaces in the pop spy fiction confected by practically anyone who can spell Ankara, Vienna, or Basra.

Specifically, we got to talking what's known as street beat, technique, training and importance of. Cities the world over all have an individual rhythm of their own. This rhythm amounts to a vague but fixed tempo, a special pace to the pedestrian traffic flow, a sense of movement residents have acquired without ever quite realizing it.

Skillful field agents must learn to adapt to the street beat prevalent in the area they are assigned to work. The fact that the beat fluctuates from one city to another makes fine tuning essential. Those agents who move through alien street traffic perceptibly faster or slower than the residents they are attempting to resemble for the sake of their own cover enlarge the margin of risk, which generally is large enough to begin with.

Anyone who doesn't fully adjust to the proper tempo

becomes less inconspicuous, more visible, a figure apart from the normal flow. The less inconspicuous an agent becomes, the more likely he is to attract the attention of resident security personnel, who already might be in search of someone who fits that general description.

Given the high-risk factor of espionage anyway, instructors from Hanga in China to Camp Perry in Virginia put great stress on tempo during the training process. One otherwise highly qualified field agent prospect I know about was switched to another section simply because he couldn't develop any feel for the beat. In the words of a leathery old instructor at Perry, he didn't have a security blanket to help avoid security blankets.

Nobody in his right mind would relate fishing to espionage except perhaps in terms of the difficulty in attaining specific targets, which are frequently elusive and challenging in both. Yet an ability to adapt to the slower, more leisurely beat of the outdoors contributes far more to the total fishing experience than most participants might guess.

"There I was riding a monumental high caused by all too many twelve-hour days at the office," said Jim Mabrey, a Chicago stockbroker who, while he quarters the compass to fish waters in Europe and Latin America, Alaska and the Far West, prefers muskie on the Chippewa Flowage in Wisconsin to anything else. He sadly picked at the memory, "All at once I had to shift gears for an afternoon on the the lake. I couldn't do it no matter how hard I tried. I couldn't slow down—and it ruined the fishing for me."

What made the experience especially tormenting for Mabrey was the fact that he managed to hook into what he still considers the biggest pike of his life. In his rush to get the fish up to the boat he played it too fast—he'd lost the flow so vital to Positive Fishing—and the pike broke off a flashy spoon Mabrey suspects he hadn't knotted to the line with enough loops during a hurried and preoccupied moment earlier.

Mabrey's anger is in no way unique. Anglers in pursuit of trout, salmon, bass, pike, catfish, crappie, and other panfish, anglers in pursuit of nothing more than an enjoyable day soaking in the sunshine often fall on hard times when nothing goes right simply because they started all wrong.

Consider the plight of a typical fisherman who's been counting down the days to a weekend on some river or lake normally stuffed with enough fish to fill his dreams. Anxious to get started, the blood starting to pump as the trip begins, he loads the car and sets out for the backlands. Along the way his tensions diminish, remain fairly constant, or grow depending on a number of variables, including traffic, road conditions, and even the law, as I learned for myself the morning I was stopped twice for speeding only a few miles short of my goal.

His tempo still in the range of the urban area he has physically, if not psychologically, forsaken, the angler hurries to the waterway, hurries to joint up his rod, hurries to swing that first cast without ever pausing to switch to the different pace of the environment in which he will be performing. The consequences can be disastrous.

Certainly the hazy recollections that pass for small talk when fishermen gather thrum with memories of misfortunes specifically caused by a lack of calm. Among a number of assorted lapses, they admit to having forgotten nets, rods, reels, and spare spools, spilling boxes of hooks, lures, weights, and flies, putting accidental knots in leaders, failing to replace frayed or knotted line, even snapping rod tips.

"I was in such a hurry to get started that I left a pail of minnows back home," a friend once told me during a long recital of the various agonies his hell-bent rush had caused. "But I guess that wasn't really so bad. That same season I drove more than fifty miles to Pistakee Bay before I discovered I'd remembered everything except for my two rods."

While most frustrations are relatively mild, subject to correction the next time an angler sets out on another trip, the emotional fallout can be harmful. Those who don't fish at the proper beat frequently cast too fast, pump the rod too fast, try to hook and play fish too fast, and change lures, baits, or flies too often. Sooner or later those lapses exert a negative influence on concentration, confidence, and other essentials.

Like it or not, we all tend to remain locked into the beat of life in which we normally function. Bottled up in an office, rooted to an assembly line, forever on the road peddling something or other, we develop a certain rhythm it is difficult to alter. We work, socialize, play golf or tennis, and even knock around the house at much the same pace.

In the case of those who inhabit large urban grids, which, in a nation now 70 percent urbanized, means most of us, the pace is likely to be quicker. More noise, more traffic, more people, more pressure, more vertical living leave a mark on all but the most thick-skinned residents. Country cousins who visit relatives in major metropolitan areas are often startled by a number of changes, not the least of them the fact that good old Henry seems always to be in more of a rush than he was before he left home.

Whoever we are, wherever we come from, then, we fishermen must correct to allow for the different rhythm if we are to fish to our outer limits. Those who ignore this do so at their own peril. While the rhythm itself is subliminal, the loss of both fish and the manifold pleasures of the sport register on the consciousness.

How men, women, and children abruptly shuttled from a familiar home environment to a waterway can best achieve a slower tempo depends on the individual. Many people find the rural flavors sufficient to slow them down. The calm, the solitude, the whisper of a river or lake, the sun fixed in a big open sky, even the birdsong are every bit as healing as Izaak Walton once described when he wrote, "The very sitting by the river's edge is not only the quietest and fittest place for contemplation, but will invite an angler to it."

Most anglers manage to take on a less hurried pace by deliberately slowing down when they arrive at that river's edge. They walk a stretch of water, speculatively measuring it for eventual casts, study its color and depth, reflect on what lures, what weight line, what special technique might be appropriate; all the while their tempo is winding down, down, down.

Many a Positive Fisherman here and abroad ingests a sandwich or some other snack during the preliminary ritual. Nigel Wheeler, an English doctor who fishes, or an English fisherman who doctors, I never know quite which, wouldn't think of wetting a line before he's unwound for 10 or 15 minutes and fed on anything at hand.

"It's not always easy spinning the dial from work to play, mind you, but if I don't give myself a little transitional time, my first few hurried casts will put down every fish in the pool, won't they." Wheeler continued to explain one soft summery day alongside a stream in the Cotswolds, "I can feel my whole mood change, feel more prepared to fish my absolute best. You don't happen to have another one of those American Mounds bars, do you?"

A few preliminary minutes by the water slowly picking through a tackle box, greasing a line, and spinning ego-reinforcing memories of past triumphs all help cast an appropriate spell. In time, in a little time, the twanging pace of a business or active home life is replaced by the easier, gentler tempo that opens the valves for essential positive beat.

"To my mind, the right speed is as important as anything else," Fred Saunders, a splendid old salmon guide whose good long seasons finally ran out on him, used to say. "It doesn't matter how well a man fishes unless he fishes at the right speed."

In difficult cases where anglers have more trouble acclimating to the softer mood, elaborate measures may be required. During the interlude before they actually start to fish, some attempt to quiet the mind by deep breathing, giving themselves pep talks, reciting favorite scraps of poetry, sharpening hooks on lures or flies, methodically turning over rocks and grubbing for native live baits.

Back when Wisconsin's Al Henderson actively fished three or four days a week right through the season he used to go into a unique ritual all his own. Once he parked the car, unloaded his tackle, and decided which piece of water he'd be fishing, he would stretch out on a likely bed of grass.

With Henderson's eyes shut, his long arms and legs immobile as he lay there, any passerby might have guessed he was asleep if it weren't for the sound effects, which commenced almost immediately. Softly, in a cracked voice with no great range, Al Henderson sang. He sang to himself for five or ten minutes before he even strung up a rod.

"Lots of times I'd still be buzzing from something that happened at the store," Henderson said. "Singing helps me forget. I sing sweet songs, most of them— 'Moonlight Bay,' 'Spanish Cavalier,' 'Danny Boy,' songs like that. I'm not saying singing will help others, but it puts me in the right mood for fishing."

One memorable day the right mood and rhythm for Henderson produced a 41-pound muskie on the Chippewa Flowage, taken on a live sucker more than six inches long. The muskie eventually hung on the back wall of his store, next to a five and a half pound smallmouth bass he was equally proud of.

More often than not the degree of flow beneficial to Positive Fishing directly corresponds to the rhythm with which an angler approaches and then engages in the sport. Unless he develops the ability to slow himself down to the proper leisurely beat, the flow conducive to the whole procedure won't be sufficient to lift confidence, concentration, feedback, and other components to the levels required.

Even the preliminary drive out to whatever waterway the angler plans to fish can adversely affect the flow technique. Depending on individual temperament, which of course varies among fishermen, a wrong turn in the road, a puncture, heavy traffic, or a near thing in a radar speed zone sets up adverse vibrations. Thoughtful Positive Fishermen allow for those and other seemingly incidental factors.

"Look, fishing is something more than just sitting there in the boat spraying the water with casts," says Alvin Louchs, a Minneapolis construction man who fishes whenever he can. "My own fishing begins the moment I start packing the car. I do my best to be relaxed, to remember to include everything I need, to let nothing intrude on the drive to the lake."

Even today Louchs still calls to mind an especially unfortunate morning when, interrupted by a last-minute phone call, he forgot to pack his favorite spinning reel, which he left on the kitchen table where he'd spooled on a new monofilament line the night before. Despite an unhurried trip out to a nearby lake, which helped induce the relaxed mood he knew was beneficial, Louchs experienced an emotional jolt when he discovered the reel was missing.

"It was a minor thing, really, or at least it should have been minor, because I had two other reels almost as good," he says. "But I could feel an edge of irritation. I suppose it put my blood pressure up a notch or two. I know for a fact that it cost me confidence and concentration. For the first half hour or so I didn't fish nearly as well as I normally do."

As Louchs and other Positive Fishermen have learned, the psychological decompression they undergo to adjust to the softer pace of the outdoors isn't always easy. Even the hint of threatening weather sometimes causes anglers to shorten or alter their customary ritual to a point where the pace that contributes to flow isn't right.

On a lovely New York stream I once missed a first, a second, a third trout early one evening, despite what I considered an astute choice of dry flies, agreeable casts and presentation, and a strong surge of self-confidence even after the last one was missed. I checked the point of a number 12 Light Cahill, found the barb hadn't broken off and false-cast until enough line was in play.

"Too fast!" a friend fishing downstream said.

"How's that?" I said.

"Too fast, you're fishing much too fast. You're casting too fast, retrieving too fast, striking too fast. What in God's name is the problem?"

Once I considered it, the cause was all too apparent. Just before I pulled on my waders a neighbor who cares about such things stopped by to tell me that the barometer was falling. In his opinion, the river woudn't fish well for long and soon we would be in for some nasty weather. So I started fishing at a fast, almost frantic, tempo, with the usual results from such a lapse.

During the trip from home to the river or lake anglers who aspire to more successful, more pleasurable angling have a chance to tune out the distracting static they want to leave behind. If another sportsman is riding along—"Good company makes the way seem short," Izaak Walton wrote—prospects for ignoring past misfortunes are generally good. An overload at the office, a family quarrel, worries about an ailing child, a stock moving in the wrong direction, or any one of a number of other factors can and do adversely quicken the pulse at the very time it should be diminishing.

Run-of-the-millpond anglers given to a rigid view of the sport are subject to the same pressure whether they recognize the significance or not. As a general rule, these people are even more vulnerable because, not being aware of the benefits of flow in the first place, they do nothing to achieve a more favorable harmonious rhythm in which to perform.

Otis Vaughn, a guide who's been working Lake Norfork in Arkansas so long he's almost grown fins, frequently expresses a sense of regret in discussing the condition of clients at the time they arrive for an outing with him. All too often men and women are tightly wound up, their voices, their reflexes, their movements, even their breathing noticeably rushed.

"If people who've come a distance are still feeling racy, I set them down," Vaughn says. "I tell them to just stare at the water for a few minutes and open a can of beer if they like. It gives them a more lazy feeling setting there staring at the water."

Vaughn admits to the fact that he's run client anglers onto the big impoundment before they were altogether prepared. Among assorted experiences rusted into his memory, an especially distressing evening with a doctor from Kansas City still causes Vaughn to launch into a blast of profanity. The doctor hooked and lost two good bass before connecting with a fish so big that even the longtime guide was impressed.

The bass jumped behind the boat, incredibly big, in Vaughn's judgment, more than 10 pounds, arched for a moment, smashed the surface in an effort to shake the long purple plastic worm hooked in the hinge of its great jaw. Quickly it stripped more line off the reel, drumming laterally, left to right, while the doctor excitedly pumped at the rod without heeding the guide's advice to slow down and let the fish run. Another lunging leap and the bass broke off, a dream crumpled, a trophy fish not to be driven to Smitty the taxidermist the next morning.

"I knew what cost the doctor that fish, but I couldn't bring myself to tell him," Vaughn says. "He just wasn't fishing in the groove. He couldn't shuck off his problems up home. Before he got hold of that big buster bass I could see his hands shaking when he was fussing about a nurse who quit her job with him."

Anglers like the doctor, who aren't able to unwind, who pack their troubles along with them, tend to inhibit something more than the flow so essential to the full fishing experience. The inability to adjust to a calm, more leisurely beat can be shattering. At its worst it can even engender a counterflow.

Counterflow is more than merely the absence of flow. Instead of locking fishing skill, technique, instincts, and feedback in a neutral position, it often reverses them to the point where the angler might just as well forget it for the day. Even a beginner not up to flipping his rig more than a few yards is filled with more confidence, patience, and basic instinct than such unhappy persons.

In the case of an experienced angler caught up in a

counterflow process, however, many normal skills are often nullified. Bedeviled by outside pressures, still re-acting to a strident urban tempo, with confidence and concentration at low ebb, an angler's judgment, skill, and knowledge can diminish until he has little left except for the rod in his hands, which won't produce what it should.

An experienced angler in Illinois who happened to be suffering serious business reverses decided to treat himself to an afternoon on a small stream in hopes that a few wayward bass might help him forget the abrasive edges of his life. Unfortunately, such miraculous heal-ing was not to be. Because he couldn't slip out of his economic concerns there on the stream, he fished lures in improbable pools, sprayed casts into bushes and trees, eventually ran the gang hook of a small gold flatfish into the flesh of his back, all because he was fishing too fast, at the wrong tempo, fishing without touching the outer limits.

I know. After all, I'm the fellow who drove that suffering negative fisherman to the doctor to have the hook extracted.

[5]

Slow Days,
Fast Improvising

ONE WRINKLED OLD SEASON an experienced angler fished, fished, fished for a brute of a trout in a long pool up around a turn in his favorite New England river. He fished hard for a week without so much as an encouraging rise, although the trout did express what seemed a mild interest by slightly stirring when a long, overdressed Hairwing Coachman came floating by.

Just as the angler got to wondering whether he'd ever be able to put another notch in his memory he saw the trout begin to feed on a hatch of ginger-colored flies no bigger than the bottom line on an oculist's eye chart. An astute angler who yearned for the epic fish bulging in the pool, he needed no further guidance. All he had to do was tie himself a bogus look-alike that the trout would snap at under the impression it was the real thing.

Despite a desperate search of the materials heaped on his workbench at home, despite stops at two tackle shops, he couldn't find the identical shade of ginger until he happened to notice a feather in the hat of a lady seated directly in front of him at church that Sunday. From the looks of her millinery, art had seldom come closer to imitating nature. He snipped part of the feather off during an especially boisterous hymn, tied it into a midge fly, hooked, fought, and netted the trout, which came to just over seven pounds, all that same afternoon.

The story, long since graven in the colorful folklore of angling, might well be apocryphal—personally, I like to think it isn't—but it assumes the dimensions of a parable among Positive Fishermen who relish repeating it whenever an appropriate occasion arises. For one thing, it exhibits the classic dramatic unities that make for a good story. For another, it illustrates the virtues of resolve, self-confidence, and ingenuity, not to mention casual poaching in a place of worship, which can be forgiven in those special circumstances. Even four-square anglers sometimes have a dim sense of property rights.

But more than anything else, some Positives cite the story because it concerns a profound reality too many people are apt to lose sight of, namely, that adversity is a part of fishing, indeed a challenging, satisfying part. Individuals like the perhaps fictional New Englander can overcome adversity by dint of their own enterprise, which must often be stretched to the outer limits if they are to succeed.

As anyone who's ever wet a line knows only too well, fishing is filled with uncertainties and perplexities. These are no Mepps Spinner money-back guarantees.

Low water, high water, roiled water, cold water, warm water, a falling barometer, high winds, and other variables all have an impact. If and when the fish aren't running well, as happens, the odds become longer and less favorable.

Hard times out on a river or lake can last for an hour, an afternoon, a full day, sometimes a whole week that an angler has been looking forward to. But many a fisherman wouldn't have it any other way. Angling wouldn't be the endlessly fascinating, endlessly diverting sport it is if the only losers were invariably the fish.

On even the most promising river or lake fishermen sooner or later encounter adversity, blank days with nothing to put on the stringer or in the creel, holes in their dreams, experiences to endure and promptly forget. Without making too much of these, without suggesting any grand truth that goes from the waterway into life itself, it is still fair to observe that these are the times that put anglers to their most enriching test. How well they perform generally is an accurate measure of their patience and skill.

Perverse as it might sound, a number of Positive Fishermen actually seem to enjoy a slow day provided it doesn't become prolonged. Nothing brings their creative juices to a fuller boil, nothing else gets them out to those fulfilling outer limits. Glassy water, a dejected angler already on the scene, brutal humidity, or a lakeful of water skiers—ah, let me at it. The darker the prospects, the sweeter the fish—once they materialize, anyway.

For the sake of their own competitive instincts many anglers genuinely thrive on adversity, then, which can come in various shapes and sizes, depending on individual aspirations. Some people pursue a single specific fish, others a number of fish, still others almost any fish at all. One man's fish is another man's live bait.

If the anonymous churchgoing angler in New England had chosen to, he might well have taken a bag of smaller, less heroic trout while he was focusing on that one prodigious fish. But he didn't. Until the moment he finally swung his prize into the grass he was a failure by his own definition.

In view of such a subjective concept of good times and bad, it isn't surprising that fishermen who produce a plentiful volume of fish still grind their reels in frustration. David Zimmerlee has actually lost count of the number of 10- and 12-pound bass he's pulled out of Lake Miramar in California. He's driven by a vision of something more. He's driven by a vision of nothing less than the world-record bigmouth.

On the River Test in England I once found myself in the company of another angler who ought to have no complaints about slow fishing. Vic Foot is a formidable specimen, big, thickset, with a bull neck and fingers thick as sausages, a man who plainly wasn't born so much as he was quarried, which must give prospective poachers serious pause before they trespass on the water he watches over.

"I kept count one season, an exceptional season, mind you, one hundred and twenty-six salmon to my rod, up to thirty-four pounds, which is a nice number, isn't it." Foot's face clouded over. "But I have never killed what I want most of all. I have never killed a forty-pounder. I had a cock fish of thirty-nine pounds once, a grand fish, too, but he wouldn't quite stretch to forty."

If there was an appropriate response to that lament, I couldn't come up with it. Somehow it seemed insincere to muster up any great sympathy for a brother of the angle because he hadn't ever registered a salmon of more than 39 pounds when my own aspirations, some of which I achieve, some of which I don't, the same as on dry land, are scaled so much more modestly.

We all of us fall on occasional hard times. Either we fail to produce the epic fish we want or else we fail to produce any fish at all. Inevitably even the most productive, most successful Positive is doomed to fail.

How long this adversity endures and what is done to correct it is what separates the Positives from weekend anglers who haven't yet begun to fish the high tide of their potential. Whether they virtuously swing fly rods or prefer still fishing with live baits, they draw on resources that aren't found in the tackle box. Once they achieve a sufficient amount of flow, once the concentration, self-confidence, and feedback are humming, they rise to the challenge with a spontaneous bravado.

With no conscious effort, in a matter-of-fact way, Positives respond to slow days by going beyond their normal limits. They are creative, creative and bold, trying different techniques and patterns, employing old tricks and fresh innovations.

Surely George La Branche accomplished nothing less than a conjuror's illusion when he first created the artificial hatch. Standing in his waders, eyes slitted against the day's light, he'd fan his rod and lay a feathery volley of deadeye casts on the water, a dozen, two dozen, perhaps even thirty or forty, casting as fast as he prudently could, putting an artificial fly down on the same feeding currents until, in time, resident trout would view the activity as a natural, God-given hatch and snap at his counterfeit fly.

Improvisation as inspired as that isn't confined to any one species, any one type of water, any one form of fishing. One way or another an artful sense of innovation is as prevalent among genuine Positives working for catfish in backwater southern lakes as among trout purists fishing the limestone rivers of Pennsylvania. On slow days everyone puts an extra polish to normal ingenuity.

Every once in a while only a sensible minor adjustment spells the difference between good fishing and no fishing at all. Until Billy Padgett got to counting to 25 before he started retrieving a silver spoon in Center Hill Lake in Tennessee, he wasn't catching any more fish than the next fellow, who just happened to be me. After he started working the lower depths on a long count, however, he ran up an impressive catch, four bass and five crappie.

"In the heat of summer the fish generally like to go deep in the middle of the day," Padgett explained to an outland angler who raised the question when he saw the stringer of fish. "A lure that won't produce up near the top can be a holy terror at the right depth."

Positives seeking the most effective cure for an ailing day often needn't be especially subtle. Californian Vince Moulter wasn't about to abandon the good time he'd been looking forward to for almost a week simply because his favorite lake wasn't producing. Despite the phantom fish, he never lost hope. If anything, it added a challenge, stretched him to his limits. Moulter knew bass were there, in numbers, if only they could be bamboozled, which he confidently expected they could.

"Look, I changed lures, changed speeds on the retrieve, fished at different levels and in different parts of the lake," he said later. "I tried practically everything in the book before I finally found the answer."

What Moulter finally did was akin to what saltwater fishermen call chumming and the British call ground baiting. He anchored his boat in a likely spot in a cove, reached for a tin can under the thwart of the boat, and offered up a live sacrifice by dumping a dozen worms into the water. Moments later he strung another worm on his hook and connected with the first of four substantial bass.

Elsewhere variations on that same pattern have produced a variety of other fish—bluegill, bream perch, crappie, pike, even trout—when little or nothing else succeeded. No matter how lethargic the fish, no matter how wary, they're seldom able to resist the prospects of a real bonanza, even if it means that one particular tidbit might cover a killing hook.

Among the many high-flow anglers who've turned a bad day around by scattering worms, minnows, grasshoppers, and other live bait into the very spot they plan to fish, few have registered more substantial returns than the midwesterner who applied some Scripture straight out of the Bible. He cast his bread upon the water, package bread wadded into doughballs the size of marbles, kneaded one on his snelled hook, and bagged the biggest fish of his career, a memorable 21-pound 3-ounce carp.

More and more anglers in Iowa and Mississippi bait their favorite fishing holes with ground chicken entrails or a sack of cornmeal the night before, so many ripples from *The Compleat Angler,* echoes of Izaak Walton, who wrote, "Be sure it may rest in the very place where you mean to angle." Years ago I watched a Bambara tribesman fish the Niger River in his own fashion a few miles from Timbuktu by tipping a pot of rancid meat into the water. Up they came, coverging on the food, hulking captain fish, three of which the Bambara quickly took in a throw net.

In the opinion of Positive Fishermen, many of whom exult in the challenge of an especially slow day, the general run of anglers generally aren't equipped to cope with the psychological stress of such adversity. Given to extravagant boasts, lurid dreams, and visions of trophy fish before they actually set out on a trip, these sportsmen have little or nothing to fall back on when they fail to produce fish, as happens far more often than they like to admit. Emotionally they are programmed for triumph, often unreasonable triumph, which is commendable provided they can muster up supportive resources during the hard times that yield no fish at all.

In view of those outsized aspirations, non-Positives who haven't learned how to achieve flow often lose their grip when the fish aren't running their way. The longer that condition persists, the less proficient they become. They think less creatively, experiment without system, and perform well below their normal standard. For the typical fisherman there's nothing quite so demoralizing as a busted dream.

"A lot of freshwater newcomers get scared if they aren't catching a fish every few minutes," Bill Stephens, one of America's leading tournament anglers, says. "They start running from one spot to the next, and when you're running, you sure aren't catching fish."

Too many anglers who aren't producing do move from one hole to another, one pool to another, one run to another before they abandon the water they were fishing. The act of hoisting an anchor, starting up an engine and spraying water or walking from one part of river to yet another, especially in sunshine, seems to diminish the prospects elsewhere. Occasionally they despairingly leave for some other nearby river or lake despite the whimsical caution laid down long ago by catfisherman Mark Twain: "There is no use in your walking five miles to fish when you can be just as unsuccessful near home."

Frustrated anglers who constantly fiddle by changing positions, lures, flies, or live baits, rods and reels, even whole rigs are actually diminishing chances that were not especially favorable to start with. Troubled waters demand more resourceful efforts than that.

"Keep your lure in the water," a splendid old guide named Fred Saunders used to advise his clients. "Keep your lure in the water even if it isn't scoring. You won't ever catch fish unless your lure is in the water."

Whether the average angler experiences failure on Lake Jackson in Florida or the Steeple Pool on the Wye in Wales, he feels increasing stress. Unable to sustain adequate concentration and confidence, with not even a faint glimmer of positive feedback, he becomes distracted, sometimes even angry. He sprays the water with aimless casts, misses the occasional fish that happens to hit. Locked in a progressively negative mood, the angler performs far below his usual capabilities.

In time, weekend fishermen with little or nothing in the way of fish find excuses to pause for a sandwich, a beer, or an aimless turn up the river. This is motion without any real shape to it made by people idly spinning their reels. More often than not they pack up and go home before they planned to, driving the back roads and cursing their fate. There is no lift to the spirits, no satisfaction after even an abbreviated day in the outdoors, no tingle of having been severely tested, whatever the results.

Yet many a thwarted angler fishing in less than flow goes to only minimal lengths. Often they persist in fishing the same old lures in the same water in much the same old way. A rigid crust of habit doesn't allow them to experiment, doesn't free them to venture into the unknown, which is a pity because success might be shimmering just beyond the next bend in the imagination.

I have a friend, a good friend, who genuinely enjoys fishing if things are going his way. Yet he always fishes the same way. On good days and bad his technique is the same. With a slim selection of lures, fishing the same pieces of a favorite lake, the usual spinning rod, 10-pound-test line, Mepps, Rapallas, Rebels, Bombers, and Jitterbugs, some in different sizes, zap, zap, his resolve loosens the longer he casts, a promising angler gone wrong. Needless to say, my friend seldom manages to improve his performance.

The Positive Fisherman, on the other hand, goes into an utterly different routine. Should the form of freshwater angling he prefers go slack, he responds with visible zest. He adapts to the whims of the fish, reaches into the depths of his mind. The Positive Fisherman resists shibboleths and shaggy dogma in an orderly but freewheeling attempt to put things right.

Hig Manning is, for me, just such a creative and ingenious fisherman. At 80, with a bad knee and assorted other aches and pains, he never tires of the sport. Except for an occasional afternoon nap when the sun is too bright or the water too clear, he is on the river whenever he feels up to it. Even when he isn't fishing he often walks a bank, intent, eyes carefully skinned, observing a protective rock, a possible feeding channel he might not have noticed before.

Any time fishing slows to a halt, Manning tunes up his patience, which is impressive to start with. Standing in his favorite run on the Neversink, wearing the motley of the L. L. Bean catalogue, he covers the water in a lovely pattern, right to left, every cast perhaps a foot from the last, lengthening the distance until finally he lifts the tip of the rod and a fish thrashes in the light. The courtly gray-haired old gentleman fishes Muddler Minnows mostly, fishes them in assorted sizes, but he does marvelous things with dry flies, too, Light Cahills and Quill Gordons, knotted to a fragile 5 or 6X leader.

Sometimes Manning stands there in the river for half an hour or more without moving more than a few tiny steps. He lets the Muddler drift some in the current, changes speeds on his retrieve, works it like a man manipulating a puppet, twitching, shortening, letting it drift again, a magic show, a tantalizing assortment of motions calculated to hoodwink even a wary fish. Manning is creative in the frame of fly-fishing, subtle, resolute, his ingenuity a matter of searching twitches, flawless presentation, and thorough coverage of the water.

When he is angling at his outer limits, prospecting for a good fish on what appears to be a bad day, Manning almost blots out the world around him. If you yell from the roadway running along the river he will respond only if the sound has breached his total concentration. On an especially trying afternoon or early evening he sometimes changes over to a Black-Nosed Dace or a Wooly Worm, which he casts with the same intensity, the same movement, the same aim whether he's pitching tight against the high bank or up under an overhanging tree.

During those long patient conflicts with adversity Hig Manning is sustained by visions of a fish, preferably a good fish, to be lightly fried in butter or perhaps run through a smoker. He knows that it won't be long before he takes a trout or two. On those bittersweet occasions when he doesn't, chances are nobody else along the Big Bend stretch he so loves has taken any fish either, which indicates that even the very best Positive Fisherman can work troubled waters to no profit except for the memories.

Further up the river Leonard Wright scoops cheesecloth into the water for some live fly he can use as as a model, tying a stunning replica in precisely the right size, then feathering it to a delicate landing, going against the literature of the sport by giving the fly a slight tweak once it alights in an inventive effort to atract a fish's attention.

When Linda and Ned Morgens aren't off fishing Iceland, Alaska, Canada, or the American West, they're frequently working that same piece of the Neversink, too. Enterprising Positives, both of them, as dedicated to sensible conservation and stream management as they are to the manifold satisfactions of teasing wild brown trout to snap at one of their beautifully tied, beautifully presented bogus offerings.

Upstream another mile or two Brooks Roberts, a a man who loves the sport beyond anything in life except for his family, looped lovely left-handed casts in the Beaver Pool until he can fish no more. The sight of Roberts casting and casting again, the satisfaction showing in his face, changing a particular fly that seemed to have momentarily intrigued a fish down to a smaller size, arching another perfect cast, fills the mind.

Where the river takes a slight turn at Claryville we find Joe Weise, buoyant, crew cut, skinny as a rake, his 10-year-old son Bill seated at his fly-tying bench. The boy, a prodigy of a Positive, wise beyond his tender years, hurries into the late afternoon carrying his prize fly rod. If he finds the fishing not quite what he expected it to be, Weise might cast a dry fly downstream instead of up, skitter an artificial spider across a flat sheet of water, flout conventional angling wisdom by trying an enormous White Wulff when conditions, however bleak, seem to cry out for other patterns in eyesore sizes 18 or 20.

In the face of adversity, even prolonged adversity

every so often, the techniques, the innovations, the subtle variations on old themes that these and other men bring to the waterway qualify them as Positive Fishermen of a high order. Confident, resourceful, and imaginative, they challenge the sport once they start fishing their subliminal outer limits.

Some of those exploratory gambits are so subtle that an observer must often stand quite close even to notice; others are bolder, more conspicuous, more dramatic. It doesn't matter, provided that the gambits succeed and don't conflict with an individual's concept of what the sport ought to be. Positives who've gone a long while without a fish sometimes go to extreme lengths simply because there seems so little to lose, doomed if they do, doomed if they don't.

From time to time one of these artful anglers will go so far as to do precisely what most people warn youngsters not to do while they themselves are fishing. From time to time they throw rocks in the water they fish.

Certainly two visitors drifting the White River in Arkansas with a Positive down-home guide named Lee Humphrey still count their blessings. In a deep pool up to the left they could see several trout, big trout too, one of them perhaps eight or ten pounds, visible down on the bottom, not moving at all, motionless except for an occasional flutter. The fish remained dormant, locked in the same pattern, despite a generous assortment of lures and live bait Humphrey and his two clients offered. The barrage of hardware and delicatessen didn't spook the fish on what was, for Arkansas, or Dakar in Senegal, for that matter, a blisteringly hot and humid day.

To the dismay of one of the visiting anglers, a rigid man with an imagination no greater than a size 16 Blue Dun, Humphrey reached under his seat in the back of the johnboat and picked up a rock the size of a softball. He went into a bit of a windup and launched it into the pool.

"Maybe that will stir them up," he drawled.

As things turned out, Humphrey needn't have been so bashful. Up they came, moving and active, stirred to a point of finding their appetites, which cost three of those trout, the best of them a six and a half pounder, their lives.

In emergency situations other emboldened anglers have heaved rocks into rivers and lakes to activate diffident bass, crappie, bluegill, and—on the Thames near Oxford on a day I won't ever forget—even pike, a species whose truculent disposition suggests that a prickly old-timer might catch the rock and throw it back. But the fundamental logic is clear: special circumstances call for special handling.

In many ways the imaginative pressures a Positive applies to tighten a slack afternoon are less important than the hopeful and questioning manner in which he goes about it. These freshwater artists try various lures, flies, or baits, try various techniques, try various depths and pieces of water. But they never change from one plug to another, never change from the depths to the flats unless they run those changes through a feedback stretched to its limits.

When professional angler Bill Dance suffers a bad spell, which doesn't happen often enough in the view of competitors along the tournament trail, he frequently pauses for a few reflective moments. He puts down his rod, stretches his legs, and unwinds without losing his concentration, which is formidable.

"I analyze what I have done and try to figure out where I've gone wrong," Dance says. "Just stopping, thinking, and studying often helps me find the missing ingredient."

In one instance that missing ingredient meant no more than a minor correction. Dance suspected he'd been hurrying the retrieve on a crank bait that generally produced for him. On the basis of the next few minutes his suspicion proved to be sound. Fishing the same lure at a more prudent speed, changing pace, he quickly produced three bass and a crappie.

The specific factors that cause a fishery to tail off often suggest the specific solution required. If troubled water is so clear that even a myopic walleye pike can read the manufacturer's name and address on an artificial lure, it's better to fish live baits.

In addition to dressing in the standard neutral or drab colors, covering bright spots like belt buckles, shiny reels, and metal oarlocks, making sure the sun is up ahead and won't spotlight the angler, Positives who feel flow unconsciously slow themselves down. They move into casting range at a gradual, leisurely tempo, remain motionless until any fish becomes accustomed to the new bulk they may perceive, then slowly lift a rod and slowly cast it.

If a normally productive fishery dramatically tails off, or if a less familiar river or lake reported to hold an abundance of fish slows down on bright days, even more elaborate strictures may be in order. In an attempt to become at one with the environment, experienced fishermen, genuine Positive Fishermen, sometimes resort to the kneepads more common to basketball players.

During a lunch break on a distant river I once watched Dermot Wilson quietly perform after a relatively slow morning. He crept up on the water on all fours and then, doubled up like a sideshow contortionist, flicked a moderately long line onto the river. He was so still, so well camouflaged, so passive even when he scored that I scarcely noticed he had taken two fish before my very eyes.

Sometimes anglers pick up a stray fish without

managing to hit the mother lode. Since several species tend to school together, such a discovery can amount to a guide.

"I let the fish lead me," Frank Duke, who fishes the Tennessee Valley waters, told an acquaintance he'd invited to join him one morning.

"Lead you?"

"Yup. The signal fish leads me straight to the school."

Frank Duke promptly treated him to a demonstration. After fishing for a few minutes, he flipped a bluegill into the boat. He gently removed the hook, gently tied a length of line through the bluegill's mouth, knotted a floating bobber to the other end of the line, and threw the fish back into the lake.

As the bluegill swam somewhere down below, the red and white bobber moved across the surface to some shaded water almost 50 yards away. Duke relocated the boat and settled down to some serious fishing in the wash of the bobber. In less than two hours he and his guest had 27 bluegills, along with two bass.

When Duke is fishing in trying times, when the fish simply aren't running for him, he resorts to other ruses, some wildly improbable. He will fish two rods rigged with different lures or baits set at different depths, fish goldfish, live frogs, even live mice.

A companion questioned Duke's judgment the barren day he hitched on a lure that might have come from a novelty shop instead of a tackle store. At first glance it wasn't specially attractive, not with great rubbery legs, a long propeller fore and aft, a pellet to stain the water a bright red. The companion was still making critical sounds when the first fish connected, a bass, almost four pounds.

"If fish won't take what they normally feed on, throw them something so different they can't help but take notice," Duke remarked. "One time or another fish hit at almost anything."

And so they do. Game fish and panfish alike have been known to snap at a bewildering assortment of odds and ends—cigarette butts, corks, hard candy, balled-up paper, rubber heels, banana peels, small bottles, even a pair of manicure scissors that the Iowa Conservation Department people found in a pike.

In view of the great variety, in view of some of the surprising things Positive Fishermen use to bamboozle fish, a snapshot still in my memory was not so comical as it then seemed. A relic of a man sat under a concrete bridge fishing the Fox River with a long Pikie Minnow built to be cast or trolled, according to the directions. The man not only let it sit quietly on the water, but each treble hook was festooned with a night crawler. I didn't see him later, but I know for certain he didn't catch any fewer fish than I did.

For all I know he actually may have caught more, perhaps several more. I was young and relatively innocent then, not yet aware of the subtle currents we fish when our minds stretch and we go beyond the limiting rigid orthodoxy of the sport. On a day when nothing else was taking fish on the Fox River the sheer bravado of that seemingly ludicrous rig might well have been profound.

[6]

The Trinity Pool

SOME SEASONS AGO the late Edward R. Hewitt, a most eminent Positive Fisherman whose prodigious skills ranked him as a virtuoso of the very first water (as Hewitt himself occasionally was likely to remind anyone not aware of it), took the trouble to classify the three stages of the angler. In his opinion an enthusiast starts by trying to catch all the fish he possibly can, develops an interest only in large fish fit to hang on the library wall, and eventually achieves a reflective level where he enjoys fishing for its own sake, with or without much in the way of fish.

That codification strikes me as altogether sound despite a certain perversity of my own. My appreciation of the surrounding sights and sounds—for example one of my most memorable fishing experiences was the day I saw two bald eagles—has gradually enlarged, but I suspect that I am marooned in all three stages simultaneously. The scent of piney woods, the whisper of a silver stream, the flutter of lark or thrush cast a powerful spell, no doubt about it, and yet I admit to wanting a number of fish, the bigger the better.

Whether Edward R. Hewitt realized it or not, his

sensible sketch of the evolution of fishermen helps anglers focus on their own individual motivation, which can be important. Unless they clearly perceive the specific goals they pursue, understand just why they are fishing, they won't achieve the full promise that Positive Fishing offers.

Exactly what causes people to converge on some waterway whenever they get the chance is often a matter of some confusion. Beginners aren't sure what attracted them in the first place, medium-length enthusiasts sometimes attribute mistaken motives to their love of the sport, and old-timers who genuinely believe they have reached philosophical heights often haven't. Large shoals of anglers fish without being aware of the deep roots of their interest.

"Why do I fish?" Dennis Fitch, an angular young salesman from Washington, D.C., who casts for bass, trout and the occasional salmon, blinked in surprise. "That's a silly question. I fish because I want to catch a fish as long as my arm. It's that simple."

Once he fell to brooding on the matter, however, as he did later, Fitch acknowledged that fishing meant both more and less than that to him. Even if he lands that trophy fish wistfully stirring in his mind, he admits he'll immediately set his sights on something bigger still, which, in his case, will amount to a walloping big fish indeed. While he generally doesn't discuss such things in the macho, biggest-fish-I-ever-saw company of fellow anglers, he has learned to love the soft, bucolic outdoors, even when the fishing is so slow he doesn't see a tempting rise.

Those who have yet to achieve the positive higher reaches of angling might say that a clear personal awareness of why they fish isn't important provided they are enjoying themselves in their own fashion, adapting themselves to whatever limits they choose. This is true, yet there is more to it than that. If participants fail to identify their personal goals they will also fail to relate the powers of Positive Fishing to those needs.

Anglers more interested in quantitative results, as millions of Americans are no matter how long they have fished, can gratify their interests only if they fish for certain species. Atlantic salmon, muskie, even freshwater striper bass are all so occasional as to discourage high-volume fishermen, who register disappointment or even failure when they don't catch a good number of fish.

As a psychiatrist friend who fishes himself once explained, people more interested in total numbers are not at all confined to beginners, although beginners generally do judge success strictly in terms of returns. According to him, compulsive overachievers in other aspects of life will enjoy fishing only if they perform very well. Those who consistently don't perform well will eventually lose interest and probably take up another sport that offers more abundant visible returns.

The psychiatrist might well have been describing a midwestern angler I knew years ago, who, while more proficient than most in the mechanics of casting, reading water, and other technique, was ready to renounce fishing before he came to a significant decision. For reasons those who knew him well could never quite fathom, John chose to fish mostly for muskies in the Chippewa Flowage area in Wisconsin, where even big producers count fish in exceedingly small numbers. A muskie, which can weigh as much as 69 pounds, the size of the current record, and measure the length of a 12-year-old boy, isn't easy to come by.

Muskie fishermen in hopes of hanging a huge shape on the end of their line fish for days, weeks, months, even whole seasons without hooking even one striped, razor-toothed specimen. A good muskie expert in upper New York went three seasons without landing a fish despite several ambitious trips into the Thousand Island area, which isn't surprising, because some people go a lifetime. The angler finally managed to kill a 33-pound tiger muskie, which wasn't beaten to death in the boat before it mangled three fingers of his right hand.

On the basis of its savage disposition as well as its elusive nature, the muskie that midwesterner chose as his target species has become the stuff of considerable folklore, much of it all too true. Probably the most familiar story concerns the angler who, on his return from a long week in Hayward, Wisconsin, was asked how many fish he'd taken.

"None," he said.

"Too bad. That's too bad."

"No, not really. When you're out after muskie none is plenty."

The longer the midwesterner fished for muskie, the more despairing he grew. Toward the end of the summer, with no fish to his rod and only a brief speckled sight of one down on a sandbar, he seriously considered giving up fishing entirely before a friend helped him fix priorities more suited to his emotional needs.

He admitted that he had settled on muskies not because he especially admired the fish, but because, being the largest and strongest freshwater game fish in America, it promised the greatest challenge. As an active person whose other extracurricular activities include bowling, barnyard basketball, and poker, he likes fairly constant action, which muskie fishing obviously doesn't offer, although the physical action is apt to be brutal in those rare moments when a man actually hooks a fish.

Instead of devoting himself to a species given to only

occasional hammers at a live sucker bait or big artificial lure, that angler could best fulfill his needs by concentrating on some school fish that exists in far greater numbers. In time he did exactly that. He began to fish for bluegill, perch, crappie, and other panfish, smaller, less challenging, but plentiful and sporting on the light fly tackle he rigged to fish them with poppers and small flies. By scaling his fishing to size, he discovered the kind of angling that pleased him the most.

In England a professional debt collector named Ade Scutt—in view of his hulking size, I always wonder whether any poor debtor is ever remiss in settling an account—hit on an extreme approach to assembly-line fishing to satisfy his own desire for frequent action. At the time he first took up the sport he considered coarse fishing for roach or tench, barbel or carp, which can run to respectable sizes even if a catch of only two or three often represents a successful day.

What Scutt finally settled on was the bleak, a tiny shoal fish about the size of a minnow, which most fellow anglers use strictly as live bait for something bigger. But by skinning literally hundreds of bleak off the top of the water Scutt—who's generally known as the Bleak Machine on the Lee and other rivers outside of London—manages to satisfy his aesthetic and competitive impulses. The high-volume angler even wins an occasional match-fishing tournament, where a cash prize of 50 or 100 pounds sterling goes to the competitor who registers the heaviest total catch weight.

A companion once saw Scutt take 18 pounds of bleak, which weigh perhaps half an ounce each, in a single five-hour match. A grin loosening his big, meaty face, the stress of his business day diminished, Scutt fishes with a sense of great joy even if the numbers aren't especially good, which they almost always are given the supply factor and his prowess.

"I like my kind of fishing," Scutt says. "It keeps me busy all the time. Took over seven hundred bleak in a competition one day, you know."

Even Izaak Walton would have been impressed by so prolific a Positive Fisherman as Scutt. Three centuries ago Piscator, or Walton himself, wrote, "I will tell you, Scholar, I once heard one say, 'I enjoy not him that eats better meat than I do, nor him that is richer, or that wears better clothes than I do; I enjoy nobody but him, and him only, that catches more fish than I do.'" Aside from the aesthetic factors, which seldom appeared to bother him much anyway, Walton would certainly have been pigeonholed in Edward Hewitt's first, or quantitative, category.

An angler must determine which particular emphasis is best suited to his own temperament and needs if the full pleasure of the sport is to be realized. A person prospecting for the occasional big fish when he'd be far happier filling a stringer, a person who's mistakenly convinced himself that the atmosphere is more important than the big fish he subconsciously aspires to hook, a person who'd actually be more content wading a stream or drifting a boat without an electronic calculator to keep count, all suffer from what amounts to angling's equivalent of the identity crisis. They're all of them fishing, sort of, and yet they aren't engaged in the form of fishing that leads to the greatest satisfaction.

Individuals who don't realize what drives them sometimes go to the trouble of developing specific skills that are of no real value once they discover they've taken a wrong turn in the road. This is especially true in the case of men and women who tell themselves that they ought to enjoy fly-fishing for trout beyond any other form of angling.

Unfortunately, fly-fishing for trout has taken on an elitist image it in no way deserves. Endless cartoons of bloated old plutocrats swinging long rods, butlers reaching into the car for the master's straw creel, chest waders and wading staffs, fishing vests and staghorn priests, temperature gauges and grouse helmets festooned with ornamental flies all contribute to a flavor that really isn't so, although many prospects keep buying fly tackle for the wrong reasons.

In many ways, the mechanics of fly casting are easier to master than spin casting or even creative live-bait fishing. The trout, especially the brown trout, is indeed a wary fish and the nuances can be quite subtle, but the brook trout is little more selective than the catfish, which feeds on practically anything, including a ball of cantaloupe I once used as bait on a lake in Tennessee. There is a legitimate case to be made for fishing native brown trout on dry flies or nymphs, a challenge that can take on the shadings of an art form, but there is a legitimate case to be made for skillfully fishing big carp with doughballs, too.

For reasons that relate to basic human nature, which is generally as imperfect on the waterways as off them, all too many Americans consider social stratifications and peer-group pressure in choosing a particular form of fishing. If those people they admire and enjoy fish nothing except bigmouth bass with artificial lures, guess what. The fact that they would find some other form of fishing more to their liking makes those slipshod values all the more unfortunate.

How is a person to choose? How does someone fairly new to the sport determine just which emphasis will satisfy him the most, stretch his pleasure to its limits, offer a recreation that both unwinds and excites him?

There are no rules. Millions of men and women are perfectly happy forever fishing by the numbers, others prefer selectively prospecting for larger, less plentiful fish, still others reach a point where they actually do fish for the sake of fishing regardless of either numbers or bulk. The most effective way of choosing the most comfortable angling zone is simply to fish the different forms until a particular interest develops.

A number of people find they can fish in all three stages at once, fish for bass and trout, salmon and perch with approximately the same degree of pleasure. In England a Positive Fishermen named Colin Trott adjusts his schedule as a plumber to allow recreational time straight through the calendar, winter as well as summer, for sport that varies considerably in mood, flavor, tempo, and action. He's equally contented ledgering for roach, swimming live goldfish for big pike, slowly changing flies for rainbow trout.

"I like fishing, like everything about it," Trott says. "It doesn't matter whether I'm hammering coarse fish hard or taking not much at all in the way of trout. If I know there's something there to be had, and generally I do, I can fish happily for hours."

In America as well as in England, Colin Trott is fairly special without being unique, an angler for all seasons, who appreciates individual fish for what they are. He and others like him fish not for the pot, although they enjoy a fish fry, but for the challenge and, if it's a good day, warm and dappled with sunshine, and an occasional fish at least shows, the whole experience can be something that lingers in the mind.

At a guess, however, I would say that the bulk of America's 54 million anglers care more about big fish than they do smaller ones or the rich bounty of the outdoors all round them. More and more people lock on to some specific goal, a three-pound trout, a five-pound bass, a ten- or fifteen-pound pike, a thirty- or forty-pound catfish, big fish, trophies most of them, something big enough to hang a dream to.

In a culture that is becoming increasingly rigid, increasingly goal-oriented, increasingly single-minded, it is no great surprise that so many people feel a need to assign themselves a perceivable target even when they unwind over a weekend. How close competitors come to achieving exactly what they seek is a measure of success or failure, which is also important in many instances, or people wouldn't measure a fish, keep score during a set of tennis, mark the sheet when they bowl.

Unless many anglers who teeter in the middle phase of the sport are able to focus on a specific goal, they may well lose some of the flow vital to fishing to the limits of their ability. The goal might be reasonable or improbable, exotic or humble, a fish so big not even a tough tournament angler would consider it within reach, or a fish so modest a boy wouldn't swing it into the village store to show off later. But length, weight, species, and sporting qualities are all incidental.

For a longtime Kentucky angler named Al Gemmer

the goal was a catfish that weighed at least 25 pounds. He fished backwaters and bayous, rivers and lakes for more than three years in hopes of such a fish. A tool-and-die maker who worked a long, hard week, Gemmer found that the vision of a truly big catfish on rod and reel gave him a continuing excitement about the next fishing trip, and the next, and the next.

"Oh, I enjoy catching fish, lots of fish, if I can, but what I want more than anything else is a twenty-five pound cat," he told a friend. "Sooner or later I'll get him, sure as we're talking, but it might take time."

Given the image he could almost feel at the end of his line, Al Gemmer did all he could to shorten the odds. He prepared special cheese baits, ground chicken livers into a thick paste, dug night crawlers, even baited waters he planned to fish by pouring in cornmeal and leftover scraps of meat. While that same procedure would bore many other anglers stiff, it filled Gemmer with hopes that kept his interest up.

One season he thought he had achieved his goal, only to lose the catfish just as it seemed ready for the net. He took two cat of almost 20 pounds, three more in excess of 15, any number of 5- and 10-pounders, but the fish he wanted still eluded Gemmer. Every time he felt a drumming on the rod he thought perhaps the bonanza fish had checked in.

Down a slope on the far side of a rural road, past

a sprawl of timber, a lake spread over some wet land. By Kentucky standards it wasn't a big lake, 20 or 25 acres, no more, with a dark stain to the water, high banks on the far side, a relic rowboat half-sunk just where Gemmer stood casting a special cheese bait one summery night in 1975. He let the line run, sunk to the bottom, lie there with only an occasional twitch as the weather turned bad.

Pelted by a thick rain, whipsawed by a wind that took the heat off the day, Gemmer fished and fished the small country lake until a jolt shook the rod in his hand. He set the hook firmly, as he always knew he would, played the tremendous fish with a confident con-centrated skill, expressed no real surprise when the cat-fish was weighed in at 27 pounds, 3 ounces. After happily reflecting on his success for a few days, Gemmer stepped up his aspirations to a 30-pound cat and started out all over again.

The fact that he managed to feed a number of friends on that fish was, while mildly gratifying (espe-cially for his wife, who had fallen behind on catch-up social obligations), really incidental. Driven by hopes for a big catfish, enjoying himself beyond any singing of it during his quest, he chose the form of angling that gave him the most personal satisfaction.

A person need not have a degree in psychology to realize that satisfaction can come in various sizes, need not be anything more than a sensible adult to relate his kind of fishing to what offers the most satisfaction. A subsection of angling is reserved for all those who take to the water strictly for fish they can catch, with no real concept of challenge, excitement, or pleasure, who achieve a sense of accomplishment in more ways than one. Probably the happiest, most enthusiastic angler I knew isn't really an angler in the classic sense of the word.

Jim is a New Yorker, a gritty urbanite who works in a photo lab processing film during the week, devotes his weekends to accumulating enough fish to feed his family of four. He boasts of spending a total of only $157.35—repeat: "$157.35—for meat during a full calendar year. Every weekend, and sometimes very early in the morning, before most people are up, especially a couple of people whose estates include private fishing water, Jim sets out to fill up the family freezer.

Jim often uses trot lines strung with as many as 25 baited hooks, which he heaves into some waterway just before dark and harvests early the next morning. In one instance he won't let friends ever forget, he ran a night line to the tune of 14 fish, five of them catfish, with a total weight just over 27 pounds. The technique required baiting so many hooks, swinging a heavily weighted line into the water, and waiting. Izaak Walton compared night lines, which he approved of, with letting money accumulate interest. The final returns might not be subtle, creative, or even sporting, but Jim wouldn't have it any other way.

Like it or not, some individuals fish for no reason except the sake of a meal. They look upon themselves as providers, contemporary pioneers, people who can beat the environment out of a dinner, which touches a particular chord and is not to be critized by others who have rather different motivations. These pot fishermen are as entitled to their pleasure as anyone else if they heed the fish and game laws, which all too many of them don't.

Little or nothing illustrates more the difference between those who fish for a meal and those who fish for what they consider richer, sweeter reasons than an incident artist John Groth recalls during a trip through Asia. On a hike in the countryside, he came upon a river so inviting that he couldn't resist the urge to joint up the Orvis Rocky Mountain Special rod he carried on trips in case the opportunity came up. When several natives who spoke no more English than Groth spoke Urdu, or whatever, saw that he was having no success they proceeded to rip limbs from nearby trees, string lines to them, bait primitive hooks, and start piling fish on the riverbank. Smiling and pointing to the growing heap, they indicated that the fish were all for Groth who, while he kept shaking his head, never quite managed to breach his benefactors' bedrock sense of pragmatism. In the evolving world out beyond God's back, as in parts of America, people with a fishing rod are regarded as people in search of a meal.

Yet Positive Fishermen who achieve what Edward Hewitt once described as the graduate level contentedly wet a line with or without any fish to speak of. They savor the pastoral sights and sounds, find the outdoor arena a comfortable fit for vexations, become incidental ornithologists or botanists, marine biologists or sometimes even herpetologists. Until the season comes to an end they're part of the landscape, isolated, alone, whistling softly to themselves, thoroughly contented in the woods and on the waters.

If their personal code seems to take on a number of curious nuances, well, that's the way things are. Some purists I have fished with wouldn't think of trying to bamboozle a trout with anything except flies they tie themselves. Others use barbless hooks and release every fish they catch. Some English and American sportsmen achieve a purity of sorts by casting only to rising fish, which, at least on days I have allowed myself the luxury of experimenting, don't rise often enough.

Not the least of the many tribal customs is a bewildering concept of happiness. For the stage-three virtuosos, the actual killing of a fish is of noteworthy but not transcendental importance. Although the total numbers are relatively small, some anglers carry this an extra step. They actually take a curious pride in boasting of what others would regard as failure.

"Yes, yes, out all afternoon and not even a look at a fish," an old gentleman told me in what sounded like boastful tones several summers ago.

An excessively positive Positive Fishermen named Emil Grimm went so far as to abandon a particular stretch of the Battenkill River. Not enough fish? Quite the contrary. He had caught fish, dozens of fish, in fact, which was why he was moving on up to a less productive piece of the river. By his standards the fishing had been so good that it was bad.

For anglers who arrive at that hazy stage, a day on a stream, a river, or a lake offers an assortment of pleasures, not all of them fish. The experience is the sum of such elements as the sweet scents of the season, the warming sun, the birds and ground animals, the wild flowers and trees, the calm and quiet.

People whose fishing goes beyond fish bring a lot of this marginal description into play during a conversation. Several people won't soon forget the day that Walter Squiers of Arlington, Vermont, got to yarning about a salmon trip into Canada the previous summer. Happily, in infinite detail, he spun a pungent commentary describing literally everything under the sun—cloud formations, foliage along the far bank, the chill of the morning, indigenous birds, the depth and color of a special pool in the river, a stand of fir off to his right— while everyone kept waiting for his bottom-line re- turns. According to a visitor with the presence of mind to clock him, Squiers's lyric monologue ran more than 11 minutes before he ever got around to mentioning the fish.

[7]

Beginner's Luck:

A Positive Sign

ONE NIGHT SOME YEARS AGO a city girl whose experiences included absolutely no fishing at all climbed into a boat and set out upon a vast sheet of water in northwest Arkansas. She listened carefully while a native guide explained how to swing the spinning rod, how to set the hook, how to play the fish, if and when, which seemed to cover the prospects on her very first outing.

In less than 15 minutes the attractive novice was into her first fish. She howled like a banshee, kept the line tight, held her rod tip at the proper high angle she'd been told to. Neither the girl nor her sponsor seated on a thwart up in the front of the boat would have bet a nickel on that fish until the guide finally scooped it into the net, a bass, a bigmouth bass, five and a half pounds on the scales.

Once she got a grip on her nerve ends again the buoyant apprentice started fanning the dark waters with her plastic worm. Almost miraculously she hooked and landed three more bass without a miss, every one of them an epic fish even by Arkansas standards, six pounds, six and a quarter, and a full seven pounds.

When the boat returned to the dock an inquisitive local who saw the impressive stringer put the inevitable question.

"Who caught them nice bass?" he asked.

"Joan, Joan here caught the four of them." I couldn't help but offer up a self-healing expression of explanation. "Beginner's luck."

When a girl for whom you have powerful feelings to start with whips a seven-pound bass her first time out, you really have no choice except to do the proper thing by marrying her, as I did, for various reasons, not the least of them the chance to hang such an ornament up on the library wall. But the suggestion that this was a case of beginner's luck wasn't altogether accurate. She was a beginner, no doubt about it, but it wasn't necessarily luck.

During a lingering postmortem of the experience later, I considered certain realities. As it happened, I hadn't taken a good bass all night despite my hopes. It's true that at the time I had yet to hit on Positive Fishing, which eventually stepped up my volume figures, not to mention my pleasure, but I'd been angling for bass, trout, pike, catfish, crappie, and other panfish—almost anything in fins—for years, generally with good results, although I suffered dry spells the same as most others. Despite my long experience I'd been badly outfished by a girl, who, however special, was wetting a line for the first time.

In replaying the sequence of that night in my mind several observations seem relevant. As a beginner, Joan was totally unaware of all the innumerable inhibitions that hedge many experienced fishermen in. Specifically, she wasn't aware that the night was too humid, the water had too much color, the wind spun from the wrong direction. In her very innocence she was fishing with the exuberance of a youngster, pure and ever hopeful, not hampered by technique or advice, convinced she might hook into something each cast.

As a consequence, she had stripped the formula-ridden, increasingly bewildering recreation down to its fundamental parts. She cast, cast, cast the same plastic worm, let it sink, twitched it some while the boat drifted in the wind. In a way, she was an adult equivalent of the cartoon small freckled boy who forever hooks colossal fish on nothing more than a worm strung on a bent pin.

Although it exists in other sports as well, what is called—mistakenly, in the opinion of many Positive Fishermen—beginner's luck has become especially well established in the folklore of angling. A stringer of big fish is more visible for a longer period of time than an ephemeral 7-10 split in bowling or a golf ball dropping into the cup.

Any veteran wetback can easily recall to mind all too many maddening instances of rank amateurs who outperform those presumably their betters. Walleyed evidence complete with dorsal fins keeps coming out of the water from the Allagash in Maine to Lake Miramar in California. Most of these fish are of comfortable sizes, of course, but every once in a while a newcomer fastens onto something prodigious.

Few cases of this are more startling than the one involving Richard Walker, probably the most celebrated angler in Great Britain, whose name glistens in the Judgment Book with not just one but two U.K. record fish. Walker was winding up a busted day fishing salmon when a pale young man wandered down to the river and struck up a friendly conversation.

As the stranger explained it, he was booked to fish that same beat starting first thing the next morning. His rod, his reel, his lures, lines, leaders, and other basics all seemed in order, although he thought he might lay on some shrimp baits too, and now he wanted to take a preliminary look at the water he'd be fishing.

"This will be my very first go for salmon," he said.

"You might just as well take a few practice casts," Walker said. "I'm packing up—and it's late in the day, anyway, not that I had any success earlier."

As Walker stood there watching, the man cast a yellow Devonshire Spinner into the roiling water. Walker could have faulted him for pitching it only a few yards out, for casting it rather downstream where the spinner wouldn't get a full ride, for not holding the tip of his rod sufficiently high. Walker could have faulted him for practically everything except the astonishing 41-pound Atlantic salmon that this inaugural cast produced.

Beginner's luck? Yes and no. The fact that the beginner somehow managed to successfully play and then land one of the world's strongest, most challenging fish called for a certain measure of good fortune in view of the chance of the plug coming loose, the line or leader snapping, the salmon surging into heavy water and breaking off. The fact that the salmon, notoriously perverse, hit in the first place was, while obviously unlucky for the fish, no luckier for the novice than it would have been for an angler of long experience.

The wider implications of that incident involve other more subtle music. As an experienced, altogether expert angler, Walker was fishing strictly by the book, a couple of which he has written himself, I might add. On the basis of his immense knowledge, he was stretching long casts out into the pool where he thought salmon bound upriver were likely to be resting. Hedged in by habit, freighted with endless dos and don'ts, he concluded that it was too late for another volley of casts.

On the other hand, the pale beginner had few, if any, preconceived notions. As a rank amateur he knew so little about salmon fishing that he didn't realize the pool would be the most promising spot, didn't know he ought to cast straight across or a little upstream to allow his spinner a longer run, didn't know that the time of day might make a difference. Unaware of all this useful abracadabra, he reduced things to a basic formula: river/fish.

A 41-pound Atlantic salmon amounts to something approaching a miracle, whether an old-timer or a beginner happens to be on the business end of the line, of course. But there was some explanation for the miracle late that English afternoon. Most experienced anglers would have cast over the short-range water in which the big fish was swimming because they "knew" where the fish were likely to be. A spontaneous, uninformed, innocent cast allowed for the fish to be elsewhere.

In a way, that experience whispers a truth. In a way, more beginners are often closer to stepping through the looking glass into the realm of Positive Fishing. Too much knowledge, too many self-limiting prohibitions can sometimes pile up to the point where an otherwise skillful angler finds himself catching less the longer he fishes.

As a group, fishermen enjoy gathering together and

spinning stories about the yeasty past. They recollect big fish, full stringers, memorable weekends. They recollect a sweet time when they didn't have to indulge in the hyperbole so much a part of the sport. After all, the gospel truth was hard to improve upon way back when.

Every so often, old-timers who wistfully spin dated stories put an abrupt brake on their memory by wondering whether they actually caught that many fish years before. Chances are they did. Fish were not only more plentiful but many of the people hanging memories out to dry were then fishing at that pure instinctive level, without feeling the flutters that can be induced by paragraph three, page 57 of the text devoted to taking Florida-strain bigmouth bass on nothing but spinner baits.

"My, I used to catch a lot of fish when I was a schoolboy," a friend recently remarked, almost weak at the knees just thinking of it.

"How many?" I asked.

"I caught thirteen fish one afternoon I won't ever forget, a big one, too, almost four pounds."

"What were you fishing?"

"Oh, a little of everything, I think, live minnows until I ran out, some night crawlers, a big red and white spoon for the big one. It didn't matter much."

"What time of day did you fish?"

"I started at noon, I think, yes, I even packed some sandwiches, noon, early August, strange, come to think of it, in the heat of the day."

"Were you fishing structure, fishing the solunar tables?"

"Well, no. I was fishing any water I thought would work. I knew nothing about structure—and I'd never heard of the tables. Remember, I was only a kid."

The conversation had progressed to a bend where I had no other choice. I asked how he would fish that same lake now that he had become a sophisticated angler fortified with an abundance of knowledge, experience, and tackle.

"Let's see, Crystal Lake, fairly good depth, gravel bottom, cold up along the walls, bass, pike, walleye, perch, and other panfish, not much recreational boat traffic back when I knew it." He paused. "Well, I suppose I'd use one of the longer spinning rods, heavy line, crank baits, mostly in yellows or reds, fairly early morning or late in the afternoon, depending on the oxygen meter and temperature gauge."

In loud, clear tones I replayed the whole dialogue back to him. Somehow it sounded even more mathematical, systematized, technological the second time around. He winced.

"I guess fishing was a lot simpler when I was a boy."

"Fishing produced a lot more fish when you were a boy, too."

The angler might be the first to deny it, but he is a classic case of the literal type slavishly caught up in the lore and literature of the sport. More and more Americans overly impressed by practically anyone who can spell refuse to breach the directions of self-proclaimed experts. If an authority who modestly admits to catching more than his share of fish insists that prospects fish only Texas-rigged plastic worms under stratus clouds from two to four-thirty in the afternoon, then a certain number of readers will fish only Texas-rigged worms no matter how poorly they do.

In the life of virtually every angler there comes a time when he must make a fateful choice. He can selectively take advantage of some of the information, tackle, and innovations and ignore others or else he can be utterly swallowed up by such things. Those obsessive individuals who go by the book(s) will never break through the mists into Positive Fishing, which is unfortunate for the sake of everyone, except the fish, of course.

Probably the most regrettable aspect of this is that it simply need not happen. Over a period of years an angler generally becomes more skillful, more knowledgeable, more familiar with tackle, water conditions, and other factors. As a result he ought to be enjoying himself more and catching more and more fish; in fact he may be less successful and less satisfied unless he resists the excess of knowledge that impedes essential natural flow.

Men and women committed to a narrow track may prosper so long as fish behave according to the book, which they emphatically do not, fish being every bit as unpredictable and temperamental as those who pursue them. If trout are feeding on size 12 Light Cahill dry flies during the evening rise, if big bass are snapping at live shiners in the morning, if catfish are swallowing chicken liver in the dark of the night, all's well. If not, anyone who fishes by the book may come apart.

An otherwise proficient sportsman in England once explained that the stock trout in his private lake wouldn't hit at anything except a size 14 Invicta during hot, brassy mid-day sunshine. He fished that prescription fly for two hours without so much as an encouraging touch while two guests decided to experiment with other offerings after a while. Together they took a total of seven fish on big bushy Marabou streamer flies not even the most myopic trout would confuse with an Invicta.

As the resident guru at a fishing clinic I attended several years ago explained, strict constitutionalists like that ought to submit to a brutal self-analysis. Until they realize that they've become creatures of habit there is little hope that their catches will measure up to their other skills. In the view of that lecturer, the most effective cure is to try and forget what they've learned and start all over again, innocents fishing for the first time, youngsters not yet twined in the red tape of angling.

Astute Positives generally agree that while technique, innovation and information can be useful, especially on strange waterways, too much of it can be defeating, too. An excess threatens the pure reflexive instincts most successful fishermen start with, as observers who appreciate something beyond graphite rods and sonar fish-finders know.

Izaak Walton cast a line of bulls'-eye wisdom as well as a line of braided horsehair when he recognized the sport for what it is, or what it ought to be. The pages of *The Compleat Angler* rustle with whispers of innate gifts that have little or nothing to do with exotic ground bait and fly patterns. His feelings on the matter were so pronounced that he was moved to write that angling "... is an art, and art worthy the knowledge and practice of a wise man."

As an illustration anglers might focus on what undoubtedly is the single most celebrated, most envied, and most enduring record-book freshwater fish ever caught in America. A Georgia farmboy named George Perry was no beginner, in the sense that he had done a lot of potluck fishing before, but he was far from qualifying as an experienced angler either, else he might not have taken a boat onto a backwater lake one afternoon in June of 1932.

Fishermen who go by the book would have been put off by the barometric pressure, the time of day, the wind, perhaps even the particular cove he chose for one last cast late in the day. As a relatively inexperienced fisherman operating largely on the basis of instinct, Perry felt no inhibitions simply because he was unaware of such esoterica. He arched his casting rod, pitched a lure up against a stump showing through the brackish water.

If the late George Perry has a need for any testimonials to his prowess, which is doubtful, they can best be supplied by the prodigious fish he hooked, played, and landed. It was a bass, a bigmouth bass, 22 pounds and 4 ounces of bigmouth bass, enshrined in the record books as the largest bigmouth ever landed, a challenge millions of people who specifically angle for America's most popular game fish have been trying to exceed for almost fifty years.

Thoughtful Positive Fishermen acknowledge the value of research, provided it doesn't intrude on their fishing or their pleasure. In view of the overwhelming volume of information produced to cover virtually every aspect of the sport (an angler I know has written a manuscript on exacly how to net trout that runs to more than forty typed pages), that is exactly what happens in all too many cases. Long essays on the ideal structure for fishing bass in the early afternoon, seminars on the virtues of the 15-foot 6X leader, even a lecture devoted to the subtle differences between the reactions of cock and hen salmon to wet flies all tend to confuse anglers already burdened with surplus data.

Not long ago a practicing ophthalmologist who spends his weekends on the water addressed an angling club. Although at least one in attendance was emphatically underwhelmed to a point of describing it as "a wasted night," fellow members appeared to be enthralled as the ophthalmologist blathered on and on in language so opaque, so professional, so highly technical that the skull went numb.

Hear him: "It is vital to realize that the trout's retina is backed by a light-reflecting tapetum. His retina has both rods and cones, but these elements are bigger than those in man and many mammals, the musk ox being a notable exception—and hence the retina of the trout has a coarser grain and lower resolution. . . ."

So much for the vital tapetum. Along the White River in Arkansas anglers whose good fortune it is not to have tuned in on lectures such as that occasionally put eyeballs to better use. They gouge them out of dead fish, impale them on a hook, and use them as a specialty bait, with some success, too, as I learned there for myself to the tune of a three-pound brown trout.

[8]

Concentration:

Always Within

Casting Range

I F I EVER BOOK MYSELF for a series of confessionals on the psychiatrist's couch, which is very doubtful, not necessarily because my emotional stability isn't in need of some realignment, as several friends have gently observed, but rather because the going rates for professional help are beyond our family budget, I expect it won't be long before the good doctor and I get round to the aching memory of a particular fish.

As I would explain it in fine detail, there I was casting a Muddler Minnow into the Chattahoochee River washing through the edge of Atlanta. It was slow fishing most of the morning, far slower than I had hoped after visiting a man at the Fish Hawk tackle shop, where I wore a hole in my American Express card buying practically everything in sight, although I did manage to overcome an impulse to add an eight-foot rod with a lovely feel to it.

In the midst of our conversation the vendor politely inquired why I was planning a trip into the backlands for bass when there was spectacular sport to be had right there within the city limits of Atlanta. He mentioned the magic words "brown trout." Brown trout, I thought to myself, the mere suggestion starting the sap rising, sweet Georgia browns, up to eight and ten pounds, swimming the Chattahoochee below a couple of power dams. Despite my lifelong fondness for bass, especially Georgia bass, which can run to remarkable sizes, the opportunity to hoodwink trout without forsaking the comforts of Atlanta was too great to resist.

So there I was casting, casting, casting the Muddler after offering up assorted Marabou streamers, Wooly Worms, and even a secret can't-miss lure a British doctor friend once prescribed during a dry spell. A warm sun was locked in a lacquered blue sky; traffic drummed along a roadway arched over the river a few turns below me. Everything was fine except for the fish, which were demonstrating none of that warm you-all southern hospitality I had heard so much about.

Or at least they weren't until I unrolled a fairly long cast, let it swing through the current, felt the shock waves sizzle up the rod into my arm. There was no doubt that it was a big fish. For all I know it might turn into the biggest trout of my career, which while scaled to relatively modest dimensions compared with the ornaments more gifted Positives net, does include an occasional sizable fish here in America or abroad.

The trout took line and pounded for a patch of weed up against the bank. I played it for perhaps five minutes, played it with great care, especially after it jumped once, showing itself for the first time, a truly big fish, easily six or seven pounds, a trout to write home about. It showed again, bowed in the sunshine, shaking in an effort to throw the hook, just when a local came walking a dog along the riverbank.

"You have hold of a nice fish here." He spoke in the liquid accents of Georgia. "You're playing him well."

For a brief moment I turned my head, focusing on the stranger to respond to the kind words, if only because kind words were fairly hard to come by back before I learned the nuances of Positive Fishing. During that fleeting attention lapse I felt the trout suddenly surge and break off, gone, captive no longer, free to swing the Chattahoochee until someone more patient, more thoroughly focused than I brought it safely to the net.

As I sat under a cottonwood tree there in Atlanta replaying the wretched scene in my mind later, I thought that while Izaak Walton's classic sentence— "Nay, the trout is not lost; for pray take notice, no man can lose what he never had"—was comforting, it wasn't quite accurate in this instance. I had lost the trout, lost it because I momentarily let my concentration slip by turning to reply to the man who walked by. I had seldom paid a higher price for observing the social amenities.

Concentration is a fickle thing. You can wind it tight

as a drum only to have it evaporate with a passing word, the hum of traffic, a vagrant cloud blotting out the sun. You can stroke it and manipulate it without any guarantee that it will withstand distraction. Even concentration-boosting professionals who run special workshops and seminars admit that the genuine thing is so elusive that they sometimes are unable to give specific suggestions.

Yet sustained concentration is at the very heart of successful achievement in many different disciplines. Unless a person learns how to avoid distractions, he may never quite attain his full potential as a surgeon or sculptor, mechanic or cabinetmaker, lawyer or advertising copywriter. In almost every walk of life the characteristic that Vince Lombardi, the sainted football coach, considered so essential has a measurable impact on performance.

"Lack of concentration on the job is responsible for more injuries on the assembly line—some of them very serious—than any other single cause," a former member of the New Jersey Workman's Compensation Board says.

A New York executive recruiter put the problem in different but equally painful terms. "Most of the prospects we place are business school graduates on a very fast track," he said. "In the corporate environment they must be bright, decisive, and flexible. But if they are unable to function without a high degree of concentration they simple aren't up to more responsible roles."

A long and focused attention span contributes to performance in a wide range of jobs, skills, and other recreations, but it's especially vital in fishing. Fishing is a split-second sport that demands hair-trigger reactions on the part of the angler. The cast, strike, hook setting, playing, and eventual netting of the fish call for reflexes, coordination, and awareness sharpened to a razor's edge. Lack of concentration during any one step in that sequence can cost the angler the best fish of the day.

When fishermen gather together their conversation is likely to run in certain grooves. They boast of the big fish they have killed, mourn the loss of even bigger fish that somehow got away. More often than not detailed accounts of those missing fish concern not just their brute strength, which anglers have been known to exaggerate some, but also the equivalent of pilot error.

We have all lost fish, good fish, due to nothing more than our own carelessness. We have swatted at a mosquito or blackfly at just the wrong moment, turned for a fatal instant when the trout rose out of the water and snapped the leader, smiled for a family photographer when a coho salmon was presumably being scooped into the net. We have all lost fish because we lost concentration, which Positive Fishermen go to great lengths to avoid.

Try to remember the last fish you lost, and the one before that. Chances are it was a matter of some minor distraction at what turned out to be the most unfortunate moment. The act of pausing to light a cigarette, reach for a beer, watch an airplane whoosh overhead, briefly exchange pleasantries with someone can all be defeating, as anyone who has ever wet a line knows only too well.

Years ago Rick Boynton learned after leaning into his heavy casting rod and firmly setting the hook. He played the fish for five, ten, fifteen minutes before it rolled in the water a few yards from the boat. As Boynton carefully spooled in line the fish came toward him, a long, thick fish, dark and striped, almost like a land animal. It looked like the biggest muskie of his career, which already included more muskies than an angler seems entitled to, but it remains a regret to this day. A friend who swung the gaff was briefly distracted by a yell from the shoreline, the muskie hammered its enormous tail once and was gone.

Angling is stiff with heartache stories like that. They come in all sizes, in the accents of the North and South alike, concern catfish and trout, crappie and pike, freshwater striper bass and bream. Those lapses have become so endemic to fishing that people have sometimes cast the agonies in the form of angling proverbs, epigrams, and familiar quotations.

"There are two reasons for the proverbial concentration of the angler," Fred Streever once said, for instance. "The first is that the fish are biting; the second is that they are not. Either is sufficient justification for paying close attention—and fishing a little longer."

Even a foursquare fisherman whose diligence seldom slips acknowledges an incidental but ironic aspect of this same basic problem. The one moment an angler's mind clouds over is frequently the very moment a fish rises, or strikes, or breaks off. These misfortunes don't happen all the time, or even most of the time, but given the number of fish a man might encounter during the course of a day and the number of times he loses concentration, the ratio seems to go far beyond the normal statistical probabilities.

The incidence seems so suspiciously high, in fact, that a few freethinkers in search of an explanation have formulated theories, at least one of them wildly bizarre in my own view. An Englishman who has been spinning and fly-fishing for a long time seriously wonders if fish read a concentrated threat in an angler's eyes and hit at the fly, lure, or bait only when his attention skids.

More reasonable people accept the ratio as just another of life's maddening vagaries, like breaking a shoelace on a rush-rush morning or losing that last dime to a defective coin telephone. Each and every one agrees that concentration—the more concentration, the better—is its own reward on the waterways.

During a talk with Lee Wulff, one of America's most compleat Positives and a man who fishes for almost any species that swims, I asked about an angler we both knew.

"Concentration," Wulff said. "His concentration has gone off."

"Gone off?" I was stunned; visions of a compulsive, single-minded zealot who seldom gave you the time of day if the fish were running filled my mind.

"Apparently. Someone told me he took his eye off a cast to watch a fire truck go by."

Wulff was being light-hearted, needless to say, but the point of his remark was all too plain. Any fisherman who is distracted by anything less than a ringside seat for the start of World War Three isn't paying proper attention. As he describes his own approach to the sport, it is obvious that Wulff feels distractions are luxuries no real Positive can afford.

"I fish very intensively myself, to a point where I blot out a lot of things," Wulff told me. "I never, never let my mind wander. It's impossible for me to fish well any other way."

What Wulff might have said is that it's impossible

for anyone to fish well any other way. As a series of complex actions played out in time and movement, fishing—successful fishing—calls for absolute atttention from the moment a lure or fly is knotted to the line until an exhausted fish is scooped from the water. A distraction during any phase of that procedure can negatively influence final returns.

In the opinion of Wulff and others who fish at higher, more subtle levels than most, it is no accident that the most accomplished, most successful anglers have developed a high threshold in the matter of concentration. No mere mechanical skill, no prize fishery, no great combination of rod, reel, line, and fly will produce over a period of time unless the participant manages to develop a soundproof, weatherproof, failure-proof attention span.

On the Manistee River in Michigan a splendid outdoorsman named Ralph Batten used to joint up a rod, unroll a few prudent short casts, pick up trout after ceasing all conversation with companions and going into an almost hypnotic spell. In England Ade Scutt, who doesn't mind being known as the Bleak Machine because of his specialty of fishing these small, shiny fish during competitive matches, admits that he has developed such a thick hide that "I wouldn't hear a gun if they shot it off right alongside me."

On the basis of his own self-analysis, neither would

Roland Martin of Broken Arrow, Oklahoma, the winner of ten professional B.A.S.S. professional tournaments, six Bass Angler of the Year trophies, and a Positive Fisherman of astonishing skill. Martin has emphatic feelings on the matter of concentration. Among other things, he feels that a fishing license in the hands of anyone prone to chronic distractions isn't worth the paper it's written on.

"Most fishermen lack the power of total concentration," Martin has said. "I'm not a normal person, in that I'm able to immerse my mind totally into thinking fish. Everything else is blanked out, including the birds in the sky, my partner, the lunch in the cooler, and the cigarettes in my pocket. I'm totally tuned in and keyed on fish."

When Martin fishes with his wife or friends, that is, fishing informally instead of in a competition, he sometimes finds that he forgets to sharpen hooks, retire a line, effectively strike a bass. Yet his powers are uncanny in pressure-cooker tournaments.

"Over the years, I've developed the ability to concentrate so thoroughly on my fishing that I never fail to detect a strike." Martin once told an acquaintance. "When a bass hits a worm—no mattter how softly— it leaves teeth marks. In the past, I've offered my tournament partner five hundred dollars if he can find teeth marks on my worms when I didn't notice a strike.

That's how confident I am in my powers of concentration."

Yet Martin's concentration has a wider focus than a delicate twitch on a plastic worm. While he's tracking the line, feeling a lure plink along the bottom or spin through the water, he is also registering other signals— ripples of a bass chasing shad some distance away, changes in water color, flashes on the depth finder in his specially rigged boat.

"With practice and determination, you can learn to filter out everything that isn't important to your catching bass while sensing everything that is important," he says.

Predictably, Martin and other professionals who fish tournaments instead of informal weekends do all they can to bring this vital concentration to a peak. They work to develop rigid attention like an artist blending just the right shade of blue or a tennis player tuning up a lapsed backhand. When concentration is at its maximum, and every stray thought, noise and sight is eliminated, Positives find they can perform no matter what distractions unfold close by.

The colorful life and times of Al Henderson on Stone Lake and other Wisconsin waters include a number of testimonials to his own profound concentration. The fact that he once hooked, played, and landed five walleye pike with several youngsters playing a pickup game of touch football not fifty yards away is only mildly impressive. The fact that he was never even aware of the game is startling.

Henderson, Roland Martin, Dave Zimmerlee, and other Positives have learned to stretch concentration to those same outer limits they fish. On good days and bad they have demonstrated a single-minded intensity that even deafening distractions fail to penetrate. Yet none of their experiences can begin to compare with a melodrama that has long since become a part of fishing folklore.

Long ago, on a misty morning in June of 1914, a solitary angler fishing for trout saw a brief dimple on the far side of a river in Scotland. Swinging his nine-foot rod, he cast a small fly tied to a light 4X leader in hopes of connecting with a fish on what appeared to be a slow day.

According to an old man I visited in the village of Kinross, who swore he had known the angler years before, swore his name was Rob Frazier, swore Frazier described it for him in great detail, the fish hit like a thunderclap at 11:50 that morning. It shook the rod to the very grip before surging toward some heavy water. For a long bewildering moment Frazier couldn't quite believe what he knew to be true. It was a fish, an epic fish, far and away the biggest fish he'd ever hooked.

Although he had his suspicions, Frazier wasn't certain until the fish came out of the water, a breathtaking sight, more than a yard of gleaming silver, and went into a leap. It was a salmon all right, a salmon beyond the stretch of his imagination, a salmon to set the church bells ringing, if only he could land it, which he obviously couldn't, not on the small trout fly, the light leader, and the line, rod, and reel he was fishing.

Yet by bracing himself there on the riverbank and playing the salmon ever so delicately, Frazier managed to maintain a tenuous connection. He never let the line go absolutely slack, but he never let it tighten beyond a faint, almost imperceptible feel for fear the fish would thrash just once and snap the leader. As he told the man in Kinross several years later, he was fishing as he had never fished before.

Frazier was concentrating, focusing on the challenge before him with a resolve so great he almost ached. Eyes riveted on the line cutting through the water, acutely aware of the angle of the rod, the position of his feet, the narrow track along the riverbank in case he needed to move with the fish, Frazier angled in an emotional void where time, weather, and the rest of external reality soon had little meaning.

In those outer limits Frazier found he was distracted by nothing. Out of the corner of his eye he dimly registered a momentary movement—a sheep, a humpbacked cow, perhaps even a deer—off to his right without turning away for a real look-see. Later, he had no idea how much later, something made a snuffling sound not far behind him.

As the man in Kinross recollected his description, Frazier first looked on the experience as a lark. There was no chance, no chance at all, of eventually landing such a fish on light tackle, but he couldn't resist a strangled temptation to play it for as long as he possibly could.

After playing the fish for what seemed an hour or two, an improbable thought rose in his mind. If Frazier could somehow manage to hold the fish without allowing it to throw or straighten the hook, snap the leader, or run the last of the line off the reel, which seemed very doubtful, there was a remote chance that he might be able to play it into mid-afternoon. He could. There was.

The longer Frazier fished, the more absorbed he became. As the day wore on he felt no hunger or thirst, no fatigue, nothing except the great sullen fish that was becoming the most important thing in his life. He fished only for the moment, with little concept of time, concentrating to a point where a thin fleeting rain didn't even register for a while.

Even the most Positive Fisherman might well write off the prospects of ever landing a truly big salmon on a size 12 fly and a 4X leader. The fish can't be turned, controlled, manipulated. Given only a thin link with a fish theoretically far too heavy for the hook, the leader, and, for that matter, the line, an angler has no choice except to merely react by letting the fish run when it chooses, leap when it chooses, rake the bottom when it chooses. The line can never tighten too much or go slack. A bit of pressure and the prize is gone.

The sun melted down over a roll of hills, the daylight went out, a slit of a moon appeared in the looming chill of night. Frazier numbly thought he had lost the fish once when it came tailing out of the river only a few yards away, line looped on the surface, but he delicately spooled in just enough again.

When the short Scots night began Rob Frazier, if that was really his name, reached beyond his limits and fished himself a masterpiece.

Next morning a herdsman and two boys came up the river from a mile or so below. As Frazier recalled later, he was stiff and sore, wet from another rain, pleased they were there to help heave his fish up onto the bank. He had fished that salmon around the clock, from 11 one morning until 12:45 the following day, more than 25 hours. The fish now hangs on a wall of the Flyfishers Club on Brook Street in London, the small fly and a piece of the gut leader hooked in its jaw, the details inscribed on a plaque, 42 pounds, a remarkable 42-pound salmon on the line for almost a full day.

And that, ladies and gentlemen, is concentration.

"No great thoughts come to an angler while he is angling," Leonard Bacon once remarked. "He is far too immersed in an immediate problem."

Indeed he is, or ought to be. Anyone who schedules a fishing trip in hopes that the quiet, reflective background might help resolve some nagging business decision or domestic quarrel puts a crimp in the sport. Either the angler can seriously fish or seriously brood on the perplexing backlashes of life. No matter what outsiders might think, he can't do both well.

A private lake I used to fish near Albany, New York, is small, perhaps a mile and a half across at most, small and not over ten feet deep, water with little margin for error, especially if a wind comes up in the late afternoon. One day a native fished it with a single-minded intensity I have seldom seen equaled before or since. He didn't talk, didn't open a can of beer, didn't even react when the man who owned the lake hollered at him a few times from shore. All he did was sit in a boat fishing with an absorption far greater than my own, which undoubtedly contributed to a catch far greater than my own, too.

Before the fisherman heaved his fish into the trunk of his car, a youngster came hurrying up a back road. He looked at the fisherman, his rod, net, and tackle box without seeing the fish, which led to a peckish dialogue.

"Hi!" The boy had a winning grim on his face. "Any luck?"

The angler stiffened, an older man who had had a long, triumphant day.

"I have five bass," he said. "The biggest weighs nearly four pounds. I prefer to think that I caught them with my own concentration and skill and not by luck. Good night, young man."

If that particular Positive Fisherman's analysis was more impressive than his manners, he couldn't really be blamed for the lecture. Absolute concentration isn't always easy to come by. Even anglers adrift in the total flow experience sometimes have trouble achieving and maintaining the required degree of diligence, especially over prolonged periods, until it becomes automatic, like breathing or blinking.

The preliminary ritual before a man or woman actually starts to fish is not an end in itself, but it can help fix the proper mood. During the quiet time that establishes tempo and self-confidence, anglers shuck off irrelevant thoughts, actions, and noises just as they shuck off neckties or high-heeled shoes. Once they start fishing their concentration should increase and hold despite such distractions as water skiing, other fishermen, and bad weather.

What helps Positives preserve their focus is the fact that they have a specific goal. Even if things happen to be slow, even if the fish aren't running well, the mental image of a fish keeps participants locked in concentration. Dave Zimmerlee of San Diego, whose trips into the outer limits once produced the second largest bigmouth bass ever landed—20 pounds, 15 ounces—admits that he prefers to fish alone because even good friends can be distracting.

But if flow, self-confidence, and the everlasting vision of a fish on the next cast aren't enough to increase attention, more drastic steps may be in order. Some people fish in two-hour units, unwinding for a few minutes before they take to the water again with their attention span restored.

Weather, the season, even the time of day conceivably can affect the level of concentration an individual brings to fishing. Men and women who realize they are likely to be more distracted in the afternoon make the obvious adjustment: they schedule their serious fishing in the morning or early evening instead.

Even fishermen riding the flow sometimes find that fatigue can set the mind to drifting. A Canadian with whom I used to fish pike averted the possibility by fishing after long restorative naps.

Dave Gliebe, the well-known tournament fisherman, has developed a technique to suit his temperament. "One of the first things I do is take the bow seat out of my boat so I have to stand while I'm fishing," he said. "This permits me to use a long rod, but it also keeps me from getting too comfortable and lazy in a big padded seat. The standing helps serve as a reminder of what I'm supposed to be doing—fishing."

Every so often sportsmen manage to hit on innovations that, if not generally applicable, works successfully for them. Bill Creed of Pittsburgh, for instance, never leaves home without a pair of earplugs in his tackle box. In case the bank of a river or lake he fishes has more traffic than he considers bearable for high concentration, he puts in the earplugs and even affects a hearing impairment to discourage any idle conversation from fellow anglers or passersby.

Whatever special affects are required to bring about rigid concentration are well worth the trouble. Anglers who resist distractions may be accomplishing more than fishing more skillfully, making fewer mistakes, and sharpening their perceptions. In terms of sheer instinct they may even reach a point where they are at one with the caveman.

In a new book from England entitled *Sea Trout Fishing*, angler Hugh Falkus briefly touches on a mystical aspect of the sport that has long intrigued reflective Positives here and abroad. Over the years Falkus himself has developed a concentration so intense that he often—not sometimes, but often—*knows* he is going to catch a fish before it happens. According to him, these experiences customarily unfold after quiet periods when nothing has stirred. There is a sudden tingling of the senses, a lift in the spirit, a vague feeling that he will now hook a fish.

He doesn't ignore the possibility of coincidence, yet he feels these eerie moments have occurred too often and for too many years for that. He feels it is triggered by a concentration so total that it stretches instincts and perceptions beyond the frontiers of everyday experience.

"By giving an angler the chance to flex these wasted hunting instincts which—like wizened muscles—have been inhibited by centuries of urban life, nature detective work sharpens his powers of observation and dedication," Falkus says. "This increased awareness of what is going on about him puts him in harmony with his outdoor environment and leads him to a deeper understanding of animal behavior. It will not allow him to cast his lure farther or more accurately, but it will help him to decide what to cast and why. If he trains himself to notice what is happening on and around the water he may begin to notice and, which is more, understand what is happening down in the water . . ."

The majority of Positive Fishermen probably would deny the existence of an extrasensory ability to call their shots on fish. But they don't disagree on the power of absolute concentration on the waterways. They have seen that essential ingredient help produce too many other, less predictable miracles that wear fins and put a bow in the rod.

[9]

Confidence:

The Wish Is Father to the Fish

During a long healing weekend with a Positive Fisherman whose skill is far greater than mine, he got to conjuring old creeks, old rivers, old lakes we had fished together out of the top hat of his memory.

As he riffled the pages of long ago, riffled them as hard as he could, I became caught up in the spell. Dated experiences spun in the mind all over again, vapor trails, warmed with flavor, memories to feed on until the opening day of another new season. And yet I was struck by some glaring gaps in his recollections.

My friend seemed genuinely surprised when I reminded him that he and I had lost a few fish over the years too, not the least of them a brown trout that might have scaled at least seven pounds—well, five, anyway. He paused, shrugged his shoulders.

"Yes, I've taught myself to erase the lost fish and the bad days from my mind," he told me. "I remember only the good times—the fish I've caught, the full limits, the successful days. It's important for me to have an optimistic memory."

As the friend explained it, he had developed that selective memory for the sake of his self-confidence, which he finds essential if he is to fish at the top of his flow. So only favorable experiences spin, click, lock into place. Negative experiences are forgotten, obliterated as if they never really happened.

Every time my friend leaves for another fishing trip he wraps himself in this protective emotional cotton. If he doesn't acknowledge ever losing a fish, ever having a slack day, that sort of inner music turned on full volume will help assure him that he is not about to fail next time. Confidence, which relates to performance in other aspects of life, is especially essential in a sport that is by nature chancy.

For the sake of the next trip, and the next, and the next, then, any regrettable failures must be interpreted in the most favorable light, if they register at all. A thoughtful angler who experiences a blank day, as happens among the very best of them, sees it as having little or nothing to do with his own abilities. He either blots out the memory entirely, which is the most effective cure, or else convincingly blames the failure on a falling barometer, too much stain to the water, glassy sunshine, or some other condition over which he had no control.

"I would have filled my limit if it hadn't been for the weather, absolutely thunderous, the worst I have seen all season," an English brother of the angle once told his wife on returning home with nothing at all.

"In weather like this it took some superior fishing even to get the two touches to my fly."

His wife, an understanding woman who casts an occasional line herself, nodded agreeably. She realized that his continung buoyant spirits helped keep the freezer stocked with trout.

As a witness to the sequence, however, I knew that this was an impressive example of an angler shingling over his fragile ego. It was quite true that the weather wasn't what it ought to have been for ideal fishing. But it wasn't bad enough to keep three other men from taking fish out of the same water we were fishing.

In speckled circumstances like that, temporary non-producers often have to go to elaborate lengths to convince themselves that they were fishing to the limits of their potential. A marvelous old Illinois carp fisherman I knew used to tell himself—in emphatic tones audible up and down the riverbank—that he wasn't scoring simply because he was soaking bigger baits intended for bigger fish.

"Confidence is the primary element," tournament fisherman Jimmy Houston says, "and I mean confidence in all you do."

The value of a chronic air of bravado didn't escape the notice of Izaak Walton; *The Compleat Angler* includes frequent references to self-confidence, several of them presumably his own, which appears to have been spectacular. Piscator often explains that he will proceed to hook and land a particular fish that he and the beginner he is coaching spot from some verdant riverbank. Invariably he succeeds, at least in the pages of his book.

While Walton goes to great lengths describing how best to braid line of horsehair, mix ground bait from barley malt, and fish a live frog, he seems surprisingly aware of the less mechanical, more psychological nuances required of the sport: ". . . but he must also bring a large measure of hope and patience," he wrote.

Contemporary Positives as different as Rick Clunn, Lee Wulff, and Richard Walker might disagree on subtle matters of technique and strategy, but they close ranks any time someone raises a question about confidence. "If he doesn't have that confidence, he won't fish the lures properly or he won't fish them long enough to be effective," professional bass angler Dave Gliebe says.

As Gliebe and others feel, confidence is a fragile element subject to severe fluctuations. The fact that these fluctuations can be caused by maddening variables—the weather, the color, level, and temperature of the water, heavy traffic on a river or lake—over which the angler has no control makes them all the more difficult to correct. Unless they put a shine to their confidence, even the most proficient anglers may well suffer.

Once a Positive does hit on a self-confident high, however, he performs well even when he doesn't happen to catch fish. He reads water like an old guide, casts longer and more accurately, hooks, plays, and lands fish with a reflexive skill worthy of his enthusiasm. From time to time someone caught up in such a state fishes far behind his normal capacity.

"One morning on the Wye in Wales I was sure, positively sure, mind you, that I would kill a biggish salmon fairly soon," a British doctor told me. "An enormous fish showed in the tail of the Green Bank beat assigned me that day. Even though I didn't have a prayer of reaching a salmon that far away I threw a big Mepps Spinner. He took it on perhaps the second turn, I played him on what turned out to be frayed line, I finally laid a twenty-nine-pound fish in the grass. If it hadn't been for that ruddy optimism I never would have reached the fish with my cast."

Exactly how an angler manages to maintain a beneficial volume of optimism in the face of at least occasional adversity depends on his own ingenuity. Certainly it is essential to believe, truly believe, that each trip, each hour, each cast might well produce a fish. In the words of Chris Seifert, the wish is father to the fish.

Not surprisingly, techniques go beyond developing a memory that rubs out past failure lest these set up a negative pattern. Among other things, Positives sometimes carry tables of world-record fish as inspirational targets, sometimes cast in series of five or ten, sometimes bet among themselves how big the first fish of the day will be. In Wisconsin's big lake country Al Henderson used to stretch his confidence by phoning a local taxidermist *before* he went fishing to say he'd probably come by with some business the next day.

"I find it helpful to count from a hundred backwards, pausing every five numbers to say 'fish,'" Frank Teller of Atlanta says. "It may sound silly, but the progressions convince me it won't be long. When I bag my first fish, I start at one hundred again."

In my own case, I adapted an ego-reinforcement device that the old Hall of Fame pitcher Allie Reynolds once described during a locker-room interview. When I asked just what went through his mind as he faced an especially malevolent batter in a moment of crisis, Reynolds frowned.

"You wouldn't believe it," he said.

"I think I would," I said. "What?"

"Well, the strike zone lights up like a pinball machine in my mind. I see, I actually seem to see, a lot of little points of light, inside, outside, waist high, down around the knees, somewhere there in the strike zone. Each light represents the exact spot where I've thrown a ball to get that batter out sometime before."

On my home pool and on other familiar waters I see blips of light too, more and more of them the longer I fish, beacons, signals, signposts to assure myself that I have run up a score right there in times past. One distressing afternoon I rationalized my failure by sternly telling myself that so many lights went off in my memory that it was obvious I had completely cleaned out the pool.

Anyone who can't succeed in conjuring up favorable thoughts that produce greater confidence and self-esteem runs an even greater risk. For optimism has an ominous flip side to it. A lack of confidence can set off a progression of negative, defeating reactions—fear, lack of concentration, irrational doubt, frustration, rage.

Unfortunately for anglers, as for people generally, these negative thoughts can be every bit as contagious as positive thoughts. They both feed on themselves. The more the subconscious sense of failure enlarges, the greater the chance that mocking, demeaning images will take an inevitable toll. In the end vital flow and feedback can be affected to a point where the suffering angler won't be able to land a fish even if he hooks it.

Fishmen generally able to sustain positive images sometimes falter when they go after strange fish on strange waters. The unknown diminishes their confidence, causes them to seriously wonder whether the new river or lake actually holds the bass or pike, crappie or bluegill, trout or salmon they had been told it has. Unless it produces relatively quickly they may never know.

The experience of two New Yorkers who embarked on a long and costly trip is a bittersweet case in point. Their spirits sagged the moment they looked out on an enormous sheet of water high in the Andes in Colombia. Despite their angling skills, which were impressive, the sheer size of the strange lake was daunting.

What let even more wind out of their confidence was a talk with a resident, who told them the lake hadn't been fishing well for several days, although, inevitably, they should have been there a week earlier when the sport was superb. Troubled, uncertain, depressed, aware of no special coves or flats to fish, lost on the enormous mass of the waterway, an emotional slide was predictable.

The longer they worked the lake without so much as an encouraging strike, the more their confidence waned. The more it waned, the worse they fished. By mid-afternoon two reasonably good anglers were shearing their casts, moving from weedbeds to flats to deep water before they fully prospected any one spot, victims of what Jonathan Harkness has called the "Delta Zone Depression."

Locked in a progressively negative mood, the two didn't even fish out the remainder of the afternoon. When the lake again failed to produce for them first thing next morning, they abruptly cancelled the last two days of their trip in favor of extended sightseeing in Bogotá.

A practicing Positive faced with the same challenging situation would establish the confidence in which to perform up to or beyond normal capacity. Given a buoyant edge, not even the perplexing mass of strange water would spook him. In his mind he would simply subdivide the lake into sections, fish one section carefully while ignoring the rest of the lake, employ more feedback and flow until productive outer limits were achieved.

"It's important to cut the water to comfortable size," Tom Mathews says. "That piece I'm fishing is the only water in the world while I fish it. The rest of a lake or big river simply does not exist."

Mathews, an angler who grew up beating the small streams of Utah, might qualify as the Positive Fisherman's Positive Fisherman. He generally has a creelful of evidence to support his claim.

Several seasons ago I saw the short, rumpled sportsman put to what was an especially forbidding test on New York's Neversink River. The water was low, a brassy sun burned out of a bright blue sky, the humidity felt like a wall. Nobody on the Big Bend stretch of the river had had a fish over 12 inches long all week.

As Mathews tied a Black Gnat on a 5X tippet, he raised what struck me as an academic question. He asked whether he should kill the fish he caught and, if so, how many.

Along the Big Bend water we had established a rigid rule in hopes of preserving and increasing the number of wild native brown trout. While members and guests could kill brook trout and two of the hatchery browns we had stocked, identifiable by a clipped anal fin, per day, it was verboten to do in any wild browns unless they ran to more than 18 inches, or big enough to feed on the smaller trout.

Since the outing amounted to Mathews's first fishing of the year after a grueling schedule playing a type-writer on behalf of the late Senator Robert Kennedy, and the prospects were so bleak, I decided that I might just as well sound the kindly old banker.

"Kill anything you happen to catch," I said, "although conditions look grim."

"Oh, I'll catch fish, probably a stack of fish, always have, always will, whatever the conditions." There was a cheery, no-nonsense bravado in his voice.

Whistling some, a sunny smile on a face straight out of Dickens, Mathews pulled on his waders and headed downstream toward some pocket water he had filed away in his mind during a brief tour of the river earlier. I fished for more than an hour without even seeing a trout, opened another can of beer for a neighbor whose score had been the same as mine, and awaited similar returns from the precinct down in the pocket water.

As things turned out, however, Tom Mathews performed exactly as he had predicted with such confidence. Fishing a strange river for the first time, fishing it at its very worst, fishing the same Black Gnat both wet and dry, fishing short range up around the boulders in the pocket water, he returned lugging a startling total of nine dead fish, three of them wild brown trout, topped by a lovely 18-inch fish.

During a long conversation that evening Mathews offered up a few paragraphs in support of the psychological advantages of booming self-confidence. As he explained it, he honestly convinces himself that a fish would at least give his fly a serious look on every cast. Warmed by his positive mood, he targeted, cast, retrieved, and played fish at the peak of his splendid form.

"But you didn't expect to take a fish, did you?" he asked me in a chiding tone.

"No, not really."

"The longer you fished, the more defeated you felt, right?"

"Right."

"So it wasn't long before you were fishing badly?"

"Well, yes, I suppose so."

A small, whimpering voice somewhere inside me had to admit to the truth of that. The longer my hard times persisted, the more frustrated, the more careless, the more defeated I felt. By the time I gave up in some disgust, far earlier than I would have in normal conditions, I not only was covering the water with fewer casts but was also unrolling careless casts, splashing the fly, failing to correct for drag, even forgetting to dry the fly every few casts. Without quite being aware of the cause, my subconscious was saying, why bother.

"Cocky fishing produces cock fish," Mathews remarked by way of summary.

In a way, my bouncy companion was merely confirming what a number of psychiatrists, pop analysts, gurus, Norman Vincent Peale, and others have been saying for a long time. Confidence contributes to greater self-esteem, which contributes to improved performance, which contributes to whatever goals people hope to realize.

"Individuals who nourish a personal sense of defeat can produce their own failures," a New York psychiatrist told me. "They have the ability to succeed, but fail to achieve because of a diminished ego."

An impressive, if not an extravagant, lining of self-confidence can contribute to greater performance in baseball, basketball, tennis, golf, football, and other individual and team sports, not to mention in life itself. It sets up a flow that sharpens awareness, increases concentration, improves coordination, and produces a greater overall effort.

Because of its very nature, fishing calls for more, not less, self-confidence than most team sports and group activities. Fishing is a solitary recreation transacted in an arena situated some distance away from the usual psychological reinforcements. More often than not there is no colleague, no teammate, no coach, manager, or captain close by to bolster morale with pep talks, inspirational lectures, or sympathy.

"Sometimes that's the most defeating part of fishing, being off by yourself, with nobody near to help you keep perspective," a Positive named Dick Seymour says. "If you don't touch or even see fish for a few minutes it can seem as though hours have slipped away. Unless you apply special precautions to hold what I call the Fan Wing Ego fly, it isn't long before you fall into bad habits."

The special procedures designed to keep spirits sunny side up take many forms. Psychological props that work almost miraculously for one angler don't necessarily work for another. An inventive person will merely change techniques like he changes flies or crank baits until he finds the proper combination. Except for depressives who regularly inhabit the lower depths, one technique or another undoubtedly will succeed.

Since confidence is generally contagious, an obvious way of achieving a proper mood is to catch a fish or two almost immediately, which is often easier said than done, and especially when the many components that make for ideal fishing are out of whack. Even fish of modest sizes sustain an angler interested in bigger things.

Certainly Richard Reinwald, a Positive of truly lofty rank, suffered no negative vibrations during his quest for the California state record brown trout on Flaming Gorge. After convincing himself that the target was well within reach, he told practically everyone in the town of Bishop that there was no doubt he would hook and land the record.

Trolling a hand-painted Rapalla fairly close to the rocky shore, concentrating on drops and gravel bars, letting 50 or 75 yards of 20-pound-test monofilament line run behind the boat, fishing six and eight hours a day, five or six days a week, Reinwald's confidence never sagged, not just because he is by nature an optimistic young man, but also because his long days on the big water were crowded with fish. He took a number of trout of more than five pounds, several over 10, two over 15 pounds.

"Every day I actually pictured the record fish in my mind," he recalls. "The picture was clear as a bell, a hen fish, the colors rather dark, one final surge before I swung the gaff."

That was exactly how it happened in July of 1971, a female brown trout, not as light as the less substantial brownies he had been hoisting out of Flaming Gorge, 25 pounds, 11 ounces on the official scales, a new California record that proved his self-confidence was not at all excessive. In view of Reinwald's past performance, acquaintances wonder how long it will be before he attains his current goal of landing the world-record brownie.

Like Richard Reinwald, many another Positive finds that excessive confidence can be accompanied by a subliminal second sight. Rick Clunn, a thoughtful tournament angler, has an ability to screw up his own optimism to a point where he visualizes fish in the well of his special bass boat. One night after fishing at little profit during the day he lay awake thinking only positive thoughts until his mind filled with a clear vision of the three bass of specific weights necessary to get him back in the tournament the next morning. Next morning Clunn landed five fish whose total weight exceeded the magic figure.

During the actual fishing phase the trick for Clunn and others is to remain convinced that every cast, every plink with live bait, every bit of trolling will produce. Such self-confidence is crucial when desultory returns endanger mind-set and threaten to switch it into reverse, but an all-obliterating focus can blot out melancholy impressions.

"You've just got to develop confidence to really work a piece of water over successfully," professional Bill O'Connor has advised those who aspire to Positive Fishing. "It's essential to picture a fish, a large fish, focusing on the lure every single time you cast."

In providing some instruction for a neophyte who had decided to join the ranks, I noticed the familiar sequence unfold. The longer he went without a fish, the more despairing he became. His casts with a spinning rod lost length and accuracy, his retrieves didn't have the same tantalizing twitches to them, he began talking baseball and tennis instead of fishing. It was time for emergency measures.

"Hold on, Chris," I said. "What do you see in the water you're covering?"

"Nothing. I haven't seen a fish in casting distance."

It was obvious that his confidence had dropped to

the danger level. I shook my head, moved alongside him on the edge of the lake.

"Your Polaroids may be fogged over," I said. "You had a nice follow on your last cast. He almost took when you jerked it out. And you can see several fish from here, a bass off to your right this side of the weeds, a pike just beyond, two more fish over that stump."

He peered at the water in search of those phantom fish that I had lifted out of my imagination. Chris blinked, nodded, smiled. While he wasn't exactly hypnotized into creating a vision, he believed he was seeing what I had described.

Briefly, very briefly, I pointed in another bright corner.

"Besides, the man who runs the gas station took five good fish here yesterday afternoon."

Could be, for all I knew. All of a sudden Chris sprayed the water with a volley of searching casts, varied the speed of his retrieve right up to the shore, fished with an enthusiastic new assurance. He hooked a two-pound bass on the edge of the weedbed and played it to a killing finish. He lost a second bass before time ran out, lost it by giving too much slack, but that one fish was sufficient.

Variations on that bamboozling theme have lifted the spirits of several other apprentice anglers I have known. They don't always connect with something, but they become convinced that it won't be long before they do, which is the next best thing.

"I figure two or three good fish sniff at my plastic worm every time I pitch it out," Jim Bates of Bull Shoals in Arkansas remarked. "No matter how few bass I land I know for sure that they're down there looking me over."

Frequently a particular lure can get to be a kind of security blanket for an angler, as a favorite putter actually no better or worse than any other can be for a compulsive golfer. Yet faith in a pet lure limits opportunity and reduces other options. A good East Coast angler swears by the brown and white Marabou streamer even though companions who cast green, blue, and purple Marabous have approximately the same success.

If that angler has caught more trout on the brown and white, it's merely because he confidently fishes it most of the time that water, weather, and time of day suggest a streamer. His assurance visibly tails off during the rare moments when he does try another color. He doesn't cover the water as well, doesn't retrieve with the same speed, sometimes pulls the streamer out before it covers the full route.

An especially persuasive example of an optimistic regard for a particular lure came about the morning an angler fishing the White River in Arkansas tried several artificials with no success. In the rear of the johnboat guide Lee Humphrey couldn't help but notice that his client's dwindling spirits were affecting his fishing.

"Well, I guess it's time," Humphrey drawled.

"Time for what?"

"Time for something I hoped we wouldn't have to use. It's what we call"—it was a stroke of genuis for Humphrey to put a name to the fiction—"the 'Calico Rock Special.' Reason I hoped we wouldn't have to use it is it's deadly and makes things easy. But if you want to take fish back to the dock, we might just as well tie one on."

What Humphrey strung to his client's line was a standard rippled spoon he had hammered flat and painted black and white. After explaining that he'd rather not share his secret with too many people, Humphrey hooked half a worm to the hook on the spoon and solemnly handed it over as if it were the crown jewels.

"A few swings with the Calico Rock Special, catch you all you want," he said. "Why not try to pick up that trout showing off to our left?"

His client cast over the rainbow, cast a second time. They were perfect casts, both of them, right at the top of the pool, and he spun the reel, held the rod tip high, sat on the edge of his seat with a bristling new show of conviction.

In less than an hour the visiting angler successfully played two trout to the net there in water so clear it reminded him that only a pinch of vermouth was required. Humphrey expressed some surprise that the bigger of the two didn't come to more than six and a half pounds.

"That's the biggest rainbow I've ever had," the visitor said. "And I've never caught two trout this size in less time. I've got your Calico Rock Special to thank for that."

The Calico Rock Special—and a surge of that self-confidence no Positive Fisherman can do without, that's the Whole Secret.

You can ask Lee Humphrey yourself.

[10]

Feedback:

Fly by Night

I N THE EMPHATIC, SOMETIMES PRICKLY OPINION of Positive Fishermen, whose ranks, while far from legion, are larger than outsiders generally suspect, those people who aspire to open a window on the subliminal outer limits of the sport won't ever succeed until they develop an automatic, waterproof feedback machine.

As even a marginal Positive knows, flow is the sum of several ingredients. Prospects cannot achieve the pleasurable degree of flow required for greater performance without iron concentration, brimming confidence, and an instinctive, matter-of-fact awareness of technique. But the glue that fastens those and other components together in many instances is feedback, relevant feedback, selectively and systematically pigeonholed, the thicker and more detailed, the better.

In the words of a trout fisherman in Michigan, feedback is the ability to pull a live fish out of the memory, which is an arresting, if not complete, definition. It is both more and less than that. Feedback amounts to the volume of past experiences filed away in the mind of the angler, who uses it as reference, especially on daunting days when the fish aren't rising. Whether it's voluminous or sparse, clear as a bell or faint, this feed-back is as important to Positive Fishing as legal prec-edents are to the law.

The first time I ever fished a picture postcard stream an hour or so north of Toronto a big, comfortable man wearing a white painter's cap came walking a footpath up along the riverbank. When he saw me casting an Adams, he politely asked whether a Coachman might not be a more promising choice.

"I've been taking trout to the Coachman on this water for years," he said. "I had three the other evening, one of them two pounds level, just where you're casting. Two years ago, no, three years ago, I had eleven fish to the Coachman in less than two hours one afternoon."

He paused as those old dimples in the water got the better of him.

"Of course you're fishing the finest stretch here, not only the slow pool on the far side, but the flats up around the next turn," he said. "I took a four-pound speckled trout on a Quill Gordon under that tree in 1975, at last light, no wind at all, when a strange hatch of gray flies, tiny, size eighteen or twenty, appeared, although the fish never seemed to rise to them. It was late July of 1975, the last week of the month, as I recall."

A Positive with a feedback machine so impressive as that shouldn't be standing empty-handed. Silently,

I passed him my rod, passed him a plastic flybox. He plucked out a Coachman, as I knew he would, cast his way up the pool until he lifted the tip of the rod and tightened the line. I hadn't produced on the new river yet, but my rod had, my rod and a feedback that had just then generated another impression to file away for future reference.

Feedback is thus not an end in itself, but a means to whatever end an individual angler hopes to achieve. It is lodged in the memory, in a separate compartment marked "fishing," preferably subdivided into sections for different species, different waters, different concepts. Some days it produces more than others, depending on mood and fatigue, and, in its most effective form, it produces with no real effort on the part of the angler.

"Most of the time we don't even know that this support system is switched on," says Chet Glassford, a Pennsylvania Positive who has given the subject great thought. "During the fishing experience we often use feedback without realizing it. We tap into it for guidance as general as whether to fish wet or dry flies and as special as trimming a little off a number twelve Blue Dun Variant to cast in shaded water with the barometer rising. In my case accurate feedback can spell the difference between success and failure."

From his own long studies, Glassford has established a correlation between accurate feedback and achievement among other anglers of roughly equivalent skills. While he admits that inner confidence and concentration are elusive qualities and are hard to factor in, the results of his one-man survey were so impressive that the subjects themselves were startled.

"In conversations with twenty-one fishermen I determined what they could recollect of previous fishing experiences and in what detail." Glassford thumbed a spiral pad filled with notes. "Then I asked each of them how he—three were women, by the way—applied lessons learned in the past to a current angling situation. The results were remarkable."

Since the anglers in his informal study group did most of their fishing in the same two rivers, frequently on the same days, Glassford had what constituted a relatively controlled sample. His people produced fish the season he studied in almost exactly the numbers he had guessed, with those who drew on richer feedback outfishing the laggards by nearly three to one.

One old man laden with angling memories, a few of them probably fickle, accumulated over more than 60 years, enjoyed an especially jubilant afternoon while three others working the same river went slack. As the man told Glassford later, he had fished a wet Cahill in a fold of fast water up along a stone ledge because he could recollect taking trout with that same fly in similar runs several times over the years.

Feedback can be as rich as an individual's experience and memory make it. Given the inordinate number of days they wade a river, Positives like Lee Wulff, Ernie Schwiebert, and Dermot Wilson obviously accumulate more than most of us, and they are far better fishers to start with too. However, less fortunate, less proficient men and women can fortify themselves with a layer of feedback suitable for their own purposes. They can conjure up pertinent details of fish that have been won and lost, of pleasurable evening hatches, of trying but ultimately successful weekends on far-off rivers and lakes.

"The more detail you deposit in feedback, the more you can pull out," Glassford says. "If possible, it's wise to remember everything having to do with a fish—the water, the weather, flies, leader length and test, presentation, everything. Who can tell when one seemingly insignificant piece will fill out the jigsaw?"

Walter Paish, for one, can tell. A British Positive who has fished more of the premier salmon waters than a man seems entitled to, Paish frequently draws on feedback printouts of incidents from the Tay in Scotland, the Hampshire Avon, the Wye in Wales, the Irish Blackwater, or perhaps the Lax-I-Adaldad in Iceland. He draws on them selectively, hoping conditions that prevailed elsewhere can be adapted effectively wherever he currently happens to be fishing.

Late one spring morning on a less celebrated river

in Wales, fishing in his full flow, which was amazing, his senses tuned like radar, Paish called a brief recess. Several salmon were showing, but he had yet to connect. What made it slightly different was the fact that the fish he had seen came jumping not out of the channel leading toward the spawning area higher up but out of a holding pool along the far bank. More unusual still, five of the seven salmon he had seen had been turned around, facing downriver, without any great height to their leaps.

An echo resonated. On just such a day on the Blackwater several seasons before, Paish had seen a similar pattern. Salmon had come thrashing out of a pool then too, the wrong way about, for reasons he couldn't quite comprehend. But Paish had successfully changed lures several times and finally gone to baits before resolving the dilemma with golden sprats.

In view of what seemed an appropriate precedent, Paish hoped that he might be able to raise salmon with the same baits on the river washing there through the Welsh hills. He skewered a golden sprat to the hook and pitched it into the pool a few yards above the last salmon he had seen. It took him several casts to produce a 14-pound fish, less than an hour to add another. By the end of a memorable day that itself automatically spindled into his feedback process, to be searched again on some future occasion when the same irregular conditions prevailed, Paish had put the iron to three salmon and had had another break off.

Anglers who have only recently discovered the feedback console are sometimes moved to rapture. On California's San Vicente Lake, a doctor in his middle years went into a lyric monologue describing the advantages of feedback, which he had systematically begun to draw on only a few weeks before.

"It's Kierkegaard, pure Kierkegaard," he said somewhere along the way.

"Kierkegaard?"

"Of course. Kierkegaard said life must be lived forward but could only be understood backward. The same thing applies to fishing."

Well, yes. Moments later, the doctor took the Lord's name in vain and pumped at his rod. I watched the sequence in slow motion, a newly mounted Positive working the rod, spinning monofilament line, playing the fish beautifully, scooping it into a bigmouth net, lifting it in the boat, reaching into the folds. "This isn't much of a fish, three pounds at a guess, not nearly as big as the one I had week before last, on a plastic worm, a purple worm, probably four inches long, raked on the bottom near the south shore, late in the afternoon . . ." His feedback sounded in splendid running order.

For sport fishermen and panfishermen alike even a

trivial factor plucked out of the memory can sometimes conjure up fish. Jane Bong Palmer, an ornamental midwestern catfish angler filled with recollections of shovel-faced fish she's pulled out of the Fox River behind the public library or above the old Paramount Theater in Aurora, Illinois, used to draw on a feedback so remarkable that it often included the precise time of the night, which was when she scheduled most of her serious fishing.

"I'm changing from cheese baits to chicken livers," she announced one far-off night.

"Why?" I asked.

"Simple. It's hot, the water feels heavy, and it's nearly eleven o'clock. Chicken livers are what they want."

"Come, come, Jane."

Jane Bong Palmer has registered better nights than that one, some quite spectacular, but it wasn't long before she hoisted a fish fry out of the dark, two catfish, one a seven-pounder, both on chicken livers, along with a ragamuffin carp, thick and scaly, which she saved for a neighbor who cared for such things.

Not every Positive Fisherman's feedback procedure is as sound as Jane Palmer's, else rivers and lakes generally would hold fewer fish than they do. Distractions, memory lapses, insufficient flow, and the toll of age can all have a negative effect, although feedback, like concentration and confidence, often fluctuates between highs and lows.

An Ohio angler who customarily does very well recalls the day he was fishing bass, bass and perhaps an occasional pike, while his memory kept spinning images of nothing but trout and salmon. Other essential components were running favorably, but he couldn't gain access to the proper feedback, couldn't take a fish. In the end he blamed it all on business pressures and went home.

Like so much else in fishing, the feedback machine can vary even among accomplished Positives. Instinctively, with no conscious effort, some of them have a clearer, sharper, more detailed memory drum of experiences than others who, while they can't draw on such a thick accumulation, do manage to lift helpful technique from the past.

At its highest, most acute level feedback can produce virtually everything about specific fish landed ten or fifteen years before. The angling memories are incredibly accurate, but two or three such people I know generally fail to remember their own wedding dates. So far as at least one of them is concerned, that lapse indicates the proper order of the priorities, I might add.

Although Wisconsin's Al Henderson never failed to acknowledge important anniversaries, it was his gift for never forgetting details of past fish that impressed acquaintances and added to his prowess, which was astonishing. As an exercise in the village store he owned he once recalled to mind just the lure or bait he had used and where he caught the 18 fish he took on an expedition up into Minnesota more than five years earlier. "And I had only one live minnow left when we came in," he added by way of a summary.

On a familiar lake closer to home, Henderson had been taking fish on a red and white spoon before a light rain began. He promptly switched over to the same spoon in a larger size, which caused a guest from suburban Chicago to put the question.

"Why did you change spoons?" he asked.

"It started raining."

"I know. But why the bigger spoon when they've been hitting the medium size?"

"Oh, it's really nothing." Henderson seemed genuinely uncomfortable. "Voices, maybe."

"Voices?" The suggestion was startling.

"Well, something like that." Henderson quickly changed the subject.

After the two men tipped over a row of beer bottles that night, mostly to take the edge off the rainy afternoon, he agreed to elaborate on his remark. Henderson found it difficult to express, difficult to explain to someone he hadn't known for long. Out in the wet a voice reminded him that he had taken fish with the larger spoon after the medium size stopped producing several years before. The recollection was enough.

So Henderson hadn't merely been fishing Stone Lake, been fishing a Daredevil, been fishing a late afternoon rain. He had been fishing something more, too. Al Henderson had been fishing the thick wash of his memory, which was paved with precedents.

For anglers who aren't able to recall past incidents on the water with the detail Henderson did, a logbook can be a great comfort. The book catalogues past triumphs an angler has run up. It can be as detailed or cursory as a person wants to make it. To induce greater feedback, a comprehensive written file should be kept, preferably composed during the nice afterglow immediately following fishing experiences.

Chet Glassford has found a pronounced correlation between meticulous records and improved fishing. If an angler decides to fill out a slippery memory with a log, Glassford urges detail so fine as to include even post-mortems to show what dead fish had been feeding on.

On California rivers and lakes, Sam Lanning, an angler whose memory isn't what he wishes it was, often does his bookkeeping before he unjoints his rods at the end of the day. Seated on the water's edge, things still clear in his mind, he uses a ball-point pen to file an encyclopedic range of data away in a leather loose-leaf binder.

Along with the length of each trout caught Lanning lists the time of day, date, type of water, weather conditions, fly pattern and size, color and temperature of the water. He sometimes adds special comments that might prove helpful: "Foul-hooked," "Pricked on previous cast," "Took House and Lot after it had sunk." He once duplicated an experience on Flaming Gorge.

Until the moment it happened Lanning wasn't certain. He had his hopes, wild hopes, if only because the identical lure had produced in similar circumstances the year before, but he wasn't sure until the moment it happened.

He was fishing Flaming Gorge all over again, on a windy day that turned so cold he pulled on a sweater. He had already fished a spoon and two new plugs with no more success than two friends who shared the boat. Despite that lack of success, Lanning, a Positive who never loses confidence or concentration, was beginning to reach for his satisfying outer limits.

"I heard a buzzing, and it came back," he says. "The logs showed the same sort of day, raw and windy. It showed me taking my trout with an old River Runt just off a point beyond some timber."

He reached into the tackle box, picked up the River Runt, knotted it tightly to his line. Never losing eye contact with the lure chugging through the water,

Lanning made a few preliminary casts before consulting the records again.

"That other time I noted that I had pitched it out, given it a few turns, let it go slack, and jerked it once before pausing and reeling in." Lanning swung his arm again. "So I'll fish like that."

It took Lanning time, but eventually a trout cut a wake in the water, engorged the plug, went tailing off to the left. By the time he was finished he had duplicated that earlier performance right down to the legal limit of trout, while his companions had taken a total of only four fish between them.

In addition, Positives who have learned how to use feedback and flow find it especially important on strange new rivers and lakes they haven't fished before. They are moving into alien waters, some so difficult that anglers won't always return home with fish, but the feedback can read like signposts helping mark the way.

Rivers and lakes are different one from another. They vary in size, shape, depth, color, contour, flow, mood, and structure. All this notwithstanding, there are significant, suggestive similarities to them too. Anyone who knows a river, knows it really well, has developed the ability to read the water for special spots—a cave up against one bank, a boulder showing in a pool, a submerged log, a riffle spinning round a bend—where fish collect in the usual pecking order, the biggest trout or bass in the best spots, less substantial fish spread in less preferable cover, the whole arrangement predictable down to the smallest among them, which don't really have much choice at all.

In view of those patterns, an angler fishing a strange body of water for the first time lets the feedback process help fix the prospects to explore. He reads the river or lake in terms of finding spots where fish ought to be and in terms of his own past experiences, which can add to the picture.

In the case of Bill Padgett, a bass Positive whose large catches on Center Hill in Tennessee are a tribute to his prowess, a change of water affected his performance not much at all. The morning he unloaded his spinning gear at a far smaller lake in Ohio, Padgett scanned the surface and shore and marked several likely spots in his mind. He knows bass are basically object-oriented, more comfortable up against a log, a stump, in a thicket of cattail.

"At first I was going to aim the boat out near a big tree rooted out of the lake." Padgett squinted in the sunshine. "I knew that kind of cover could mean a bass or two if I fished it right. But when I looked down in the water not far beyond the end of the pier I saw a pile of brush on the bottom."

Although the brush was close to the pier, close to the grinding sound of engines kicking to a start, he remembered a similar scene just off another pier in the past, which he had successfully fished. He proceeded to successfully fish the Ohio replica everyone else had passed by: two bass, neither very big, but two bass all the same.

"If I hadn't remembered the other time I would have driven the boat to the skeleton tree first thing," Padgett said later. "But when I fish I keep remembering little things. Those little things save me lots of times."

After he achieved full flow that day, Padgett was only dimly aware of reacting to specific suggestions that his feedback kept shuffling up. He took two more bass around the tree, another by adding a strip of pork rind he remembered using on a previous trip, a last fish on the same yellow popper responsible for a three-pounder one twilight several weeks earlier.

No two Positives, not even Padgett and his closest fishing friend, ever agree on every tactic, every technique, every concept, which is probably a good thing, or conversation in some nearby tavern wouldn't be as stimulating as it is at the end of a long day. Wise and experienced anglers may argue the 5X versus the 6X leader, the Rebel versus the Bomber, the mid-day sun versus a speckled day for muskie, but they close ranks on the values of feedback.

They know that even normally reliable memories are apt to cloud over when a particular waterway undergoes a change. When the Mississippi rose until it finally reached an all-time peak several years ago, for example, natives able to fish their limits automatically dropped back into their experience for a sign. Some had memories of very good fishing in high waters, others of little or no success at all; both impressions might have been absolutely accurate.

Tom Bourrett of Hanover, Illinois, was one angler who associated high water with very good fishing. So he worked the muddy, surging Mississippi at the top of its rise. He will probably fish it hard again next time it reaches flood proportions, too. Tom can draw on an impressive memory, 40 pounds on its big blunt nose, a catfish big enough to feed the neighborhood.

In Vermont a trout fisherman of some reputation has marvelous feedback accumulated on different waters. Sometimes a faint smile comes over him and he abruptly changes flies or fishes at a different speed.

On an otherwise lovely afternoon when he and a friend had failed to take a fish the friend noticed him begin to smile. Memories rose in his mind, quicksilver trout on the Roaring Branch or Rangeley in Maine, bigger fish in New Hampshire, New York, and Canada, a chorus of fish now dead and gone. He quickly changed to a tiny Adams, fanned it into a riffle, smiled even more as a 15-inch trout materialized.

So Positive feedback consists of times gone by,

times whose edges have begun to curl. For anglers this crucial resource is always available, filtered, wound into memory, lodged beyond the rim of everyday awareness, something to be exploited whenever the need arises.

The many experiences that contribute to good working feedback are personal, most of them, memories to feed on some afternoon or early evening along the river. The most relevant and useful of these are often set to conversation in the company of brothers and sisters of the angle, although examples have been known to occur in milieus not ideal for such subtle detail.

At a black-tie dinner party I once attended, a New Yorker got to recollecting a trip out to the Gunnison several seasons before. Once the memories began rising he found it difficult to stop. He described the color, depth, temperature, and flow of the water, the slick on the rocks, the fly hatches, exactly where the good trout lay in the stretch he fished, even the reason why they were acting bashful before he tied on a big White Wulff, which he proceeded to describe in infinite detail—good stuff, I thought to myself, a vivid account of a trying but ultimately triumphant time on one of the prize rivers.

He carried on at what struck me as no more than reasonable length, until a woman seated directly across the table, who didn't—God help her—happen to fish, sweetly raised her voice.

"You have a good memory for fish," she said.

"Yes, I suppose I do," he said.

"Do you have an equally good memory for anything else?"

He thought for a moment.

"Yes, I do."

"And what might that be?"

"Well, I have a good memory of just why"—he produced a name she knew only too well—"left his wife and kids for two weeks last summer."

"Oh."

Afterword

IT IS EASY TO PICTURE the waterways brightly colored with anglers in pursuit of their particular goals. They swing their rods on the Boulder and the Manistee, Bull Shoals and the Manifold, while on thousands of other less celebrated rivers and lakes other anglers seek their own pleasure, and either fail for a while or else feel their bodies tingle as good fish catch hold.

Positive Fishermen and non-Positives alike know only too well that angling is a fickle sport. There are no absolutes, no magical flies or lures that always produce, no pools or holes where fish are always to be taken. What might succeed four times will fail the fifth no matter how far a participant might reach into his outer limits.

Nothing, not even Positive Fishing of the highest order, can ever turn this lovely perplexing sport into an assembly-line exercise that stamps out so many units per day. But it does offer up a sort of limited warranty that makes the extra effort worthwhile.

Anyone who fishes in a Positive way, who develops utter concentration and confidence, produces proper feedback and the total flow experience, will come far closer to achieving his goals than he would otherwise. In addition, the great innate pleasures of the sport, which are too often stunted by an obsession with technique, can't help but be enhanced.

Inevitably, those anglers who choose mind over matter out on the water will find it difficult to bring a maximum of all the essential resources to bear at all times. Some may generate tremendous concentration without an adequate level of confidence, others may improve feedback only to remain overly preoccupied with mechanical skills.

Much as people strive for every last component that will bring about a fully operational Positive Fishing experience, we all of us sometimes lapse in one way or another. We come close to arriving at the outer limits, but we backslide every once in a while, to breach one of the informal rules of the subliminal game.

In my own case, for instance, I sometimes lapse by embroidering on reality in my imagination, although I keep these moments strictly to myself. The trouble is that I yearn to fish a number of eminent waters here in America and elsewhere, some of which I have fished already, some of which I have not, more rivers and lakes than limited time and budget will allow. The whisper of bright waters holds me in thrall.

As a compulsive Positive, I seldom find it difficult to feed on the keepnet of my mind despite knowing that I should not. If I haven't fished some epic water in reality, I may have fished it in my imagination, always successfully, needless to say. In the imagination the water level is always ideal, the barometric fluctuations exactly right, and while fish don't hammer at every cast—fishing must be challenging, else it would lose its bite for the fisherman as well as the fish—they do rise more often than not, which is all right too, if only to help balance out those real-life busted days. A grown man who's experienced occasional blanks roving distant waters can't be blamed for lining his daydreams with gold, can he?

Every so often they blur together, the sweet waters I have already fished and those I haven't, satisfying memories and wistful visions, fact and fancy, until in the end it is sometimes difficult to separate one from the other.

In the mind's eye I picture myself applying Positive Fishing on Iceland's splendid salmon rivers, for instance, the Lax-I-Adaldad and the Grimsá. Somehow I prefer the Grimsá, where I often hang a fish almost any time I want. My most stirring fantasy is the morning I cast a fly to a fish showing not 50 feet away.

During a fairly slow retrieve, the fly moves just below the surface, a bolt of lightning hits, catching hold, running a live current through the rod to my shoulder blade. The salmon feels truly hooked, stripping line, piling up the channel, a great invisible shape surging in the river.

I am in total control despite its colossal size, using just the right amount of pressure, concentrating as never before, nimbly moving upriver along the slick lava bottom, turning the salmon before it reaches a wash of ominously heavy water. Even the ghillie feels compelled to applaud a client fishing those impressive outer limits, and two cars drumming along a near roadway pause to watch.

Abruptly the fish rises, arches out of the water, almost doubles in the light, falling back with an angry smashing sound. It jumps again in rocket bursts, putting an alarming strain on the long rod, and later, perhaps 30 minutes later, lies heaving in the shallows, 35 pounds, 40, 45, whatever I choose to make it. I never know for certain, because I unhook the salmon and leave him there in the Grimsá—noblesse oblige, a reward for impressive valor in the face of superior odds. In the vapor trails of make-believe I often parole fish I seldom, if ever, would release in real life.

From all these giddy fantasies I invariably return to reality, to my beloved home waters, to the rolling Catskills in New York, to the Neversink River a few turns below a covered wooden bridge, where I fish the evening rise at Big Bend, the Gordon Run, and the Middle Dam with Bob Portner. There we sit, two good friends, two brothers of the angle pleasantly adrift in a world that otherwise seems out of joint.

Even if we don't catch all we hope to, we are caught in a tantalizing spell that is difficult to resist. As Positive Fishermen who have discovered the intriguing far side of the lovely old pastime, we know, know for certain, that John Steinbeck was not exaggerating by so much as a syllable when he cast his own testimonial for fellow anglers to warm themselves by.

"Here is no sentiment, no contest, no grandeur, no economics," he wrote. "From the sanctity of this occupation, a man may emerge refreshed and in control of his own soul. He is not idle. He is fishing, alone with himself in dignity and peace. It seems a very precious thing to me."